Addition and Subtraction Workbook 2nd Grade

This book belongs to:

_____

All students should be given the opportunity to learn and meet grade-specific math standards. Students learn math concepts one step at a time. Each concept must be thoroughly understood before moving on to the next step. These practice tests can help students really understand a concept before taking the next step.

Repetitive practice tests serve to reinforce math concepts for each grade level.

Students who do more brain exercise can develop the skills to be amazing.

PAPER CROW

Table Of Contents

Solutions At The Back Of The Book

1) 40 + 19

2) 32 + 30

3) 11 + 13

4) 20 + 14

5) 12 + 37

6) 12 + 31

7) 25 + 40

8) 12 + 33

9) 30 + 26

10) 19 + 40

11) 10 + 36

12) 12 + 26

13) 32 + 17

14) 22 + 12

15) 25 + 11

16) 20 + 23

17) 22 + 20

18) 31 + 12

19) 40 + 37

20) 20 + 25

21) 28 + 11

22) 36 + 11

23) 34 + 20

24) 21 + 26

25) 21 + 40

26) 11 + 30

27) 30 + 40

28) 13 + 34

29) 35 + 24

30) 29 + 20

31) 40 + 18

32) 32 + 11

33) 26 + 23

34) 20 + 10

35) 32 + 15

36) 25 + 10

37) 10 + 26

38) 11 + 26

39) 37 + 10

40) 11 + 21

41) 40 + 36

42) 10 + 23

43) 32 + 33

44) 13 + 35

45) 11 + 22

46) 30 + 22

47) 30 + 39

48) 32 + 37

49) 32 + 31

50) 10 + 32

51) 13 + 26

52) 33 + 25

53) 11 + 20

54) 40 + 24

55) 32 + 10

56) 35 + 14

57) 22 + 22

58) 34 + 22

59) 24 + 10

60) 31 + 16

1) 40 + 35
2) 32 + 29
3) 22 + 31
4) 12 + 38
5) 31 + 12
6) 30 + 38

7) 29 + 11
8) 30 + 39
9) 33 + 12
10) 15 + 38
11) 31 + 13
12) 40 + 12

13) 30 + 28
14) 11 + 26
15) 13 + 40
16) 40 + 27
17) 15 + 24
18) 22 + 13

19) 12 + 18
20) 38 + 13
21) 12 + 39
22) 28 + 19
23) 28 + 20
24) 11 + 22

25) 34 + 40
26) 40 + 13
27) 40 + 31
28) 26 + 14
29) 22 + 28
30) 29 + 10

31) 26 + 23
32) 37 + 19
33) 22 + 37
34) 37 + 16
35) 37 + 38
36) 26 + 38

37) 28 + 23
38) 23 + 11
39) 25 + 23
40) 19 + 29
41) 29 + 28
42) 12 + 22

43) 13 + 23
44) 12 + 15
45) 17 + 27
46) 23 + 14
47) 16 + 22
48) 14 + 11

49) 23 + 24
50) 37 + 29
51) 31 + 13
52) 33 + 15
53) 15 + 16
54) 22 + 40

55) 26 + 35
56) 35 + 15
57) 32 + 26
58) 22 + 27
59) 21 + 33
60) 28 + 30

1) 16
  + 12

2) 24
  + 31

3) 12
  + 36

4) 13
  + 36

5) 18
  + 12

6) 26
  + 12

7) 16
  + 14

8) 40
  + 22

9) 28
  + 16

10) 28
  + 22

11) 25
  + 16

12) 22
  + 21

13) 12
  + 27

14) 31
  + 25

15) 40
  + 33

16) 22
  + 29

17) 31
  + 27

18) 13
  + 26

19) 36
  + 11

20) 15
  + 22

21) 28
  + 38

22) 24
  + 29

23) 24
  + 11

24) 25
  + 24

25) 24
  + 28

26) 10
  + 32

27) 16
  + 34

28) 36
  + 28

29) 10
  + 40

30) 34
  + 24

31) 19
  + 31

32) 37
  + 26

33) 39
  + 37

34) 11
  + 34

35) 30
  + 20

36) 24
  + 13

37) 40
  + 40

38) 12
  + 18

39) 39
  + 22

40) 16
  + 31

41) 18
  + 38

42) 21
  + 32

43) 16
  + 20

44) 10
  + 33

45) 13
  + 23

46) 37
  + 14

47) 19
  + 14

48) 16
  + 38

49) 11
  + 32

50) 10
  + 26

51) 39
  + 22

52) 13
  + 18

53) 10
  + 18

54) 26
  + 17

55) 22
  + 35

56) 20
  + 28

57) 35
  + 15

58) 35
  + 22

59) 27
  + 29

60) 11
  + 18

1) 39 + 11

2) 40 + 31

3) 33 + 10

4) 23 + 25

5) 37 + 40

6) 17 + 19

7) 36 + 13

8) 28 + 40

9) 28 + 14

10) 22 + 35

11) 20 + 10

12) 37 + 33

13) 30 + 35

14) 30 + 32

15) 11 + 40

16) 13 + 21

17) 14 + 25

18) 24 + 24

19) 29 + 11

20) 18 + 33

21) 27 + 34

22) 16 + 19

23) 22 + 29

24) 10 + 22

25) 15 + 29

26) 39 + 28

27) 16 + 25

28) 23 + 25

29) 36 + 12

30) 33 + 27

31) 38 + 38

32) 30 + 27

33) 28 + 30

34) 30 + 37

35) 36 + 29

36) 15 + 40

37) 39 + 22

38) 17 + 27

39) 24 + 20

40) 28 + 31

41) 24 + 10

42) 10 + 19

43) 14 + 34

44) 28 + 40

45) 29 + 25

46) 13 + 21

47) 25 + 36

48) 10 + 16

49) 15 + 40

50) 22 + 24

51) 22 + 18

52) 36 + 19

53) 30 + 11

54) 38 + 12

55) 36 + 33

56) 35 + 37

57) 40 + 31

58) 18 + 21

59) 17 + 25

60) 20 + 11

1) 26 + 37

2) 30 + 34

3) 29 + 39

4) 38 + 38

5) 31 + 12

6) 21 + 28

7) 25 + 35

8) 11 + 10

9) 34 + 12

10) 25 + 24

11) 28 + 24

12) 24 + 13

13) 21 + 23

14) 11 + 37

15) 34 + 20

16) 31 + 14

17) 19 + 15

18) 14 + 13

19) 37 + 30

20) 11 + 19

21) 13 + 13

22) 11 + 14

23) 31 + 11

24) 14 + 12

25) 15 + 35

26) 36 + 25

27) 20 + 20

28) 11 + 39

29) 25 + 27

30) 26 + 30

31) 34 + 11

32) 28 + 27

33) 27 + 20

34) 37 + 35

35) 30 + 18

36) 40 + 37

37) 27 + 28

38) 37 + 33

39) 33 + 24

40) 32 + 29

41) 17 + 24

42) 24 + 15

43) 29 + 10

44) 33 + 29

45) 18 + 17

46) 10 + 13

47) 26 + 19

48) 34 + 30

49) 40 + 10

50) 36 + 19

51) 34 + 17

52) 22 + 18

53) 10 + 13

54) 36 + 25

55) 29 + 15

56) 36 + 35

57) 18 + 15

58) 19 + 16

59) 15 + 25

60) 31 + 35

1)
```
   26
+ [  ]
  38
```

2)
```
  [  ]
+  27
   59
```

3)
```
   34
+ [  ]
   74
```

4)
```
  [  ]
+  30
   47
```

5)
```
   12
+ [  ]
   37
```

6)
```
  [  ]
+  19
   50
```

7)
```
   32
+ [  ]
   58
```

8)
```
  [  ]
+  31
   48
```

9)
```
   36
+ [  ]
   76
```

10)
```
  [  ]
+  27
   64
```

11)
```
   33
+ [  ]
   69
```

12)
```
  [  ]
+  27
   38
```

13)
```
   23
+ [  ]
   46
```

14)
```
  [  ]
+  36
   65
```

15)
```
   12
+ [  ]
   36
```

16)
```
  [  ]
+  30
   46
```

17)
```
   35
+ [  ]
   51
```

18)
```
  [  ]
+  28
   65
```

19)
```
   18
+ [  ]
   29
```

20)
```
  [  ]
+  25
   42
```

21)
```
   39
+ [  ]
   56
```

22)
```
  [  ]
+  25
   45
```

23)
```
   19
+ [  ]
   45
```

24)
```
  [  ]
+  10
   32
```

25)
```
   29
+ [  ]
   60
```

26)
```
  [  ]
+  23
   60
```

27)
```
   15
+ [  ]
   42
```

28)
```
  [  ]
+  14
   54
```

29)
```
   17
+ [  ]
   37
```

30)
```
  [  ]
+  25
   47
```

31)
```
   18
+ [  ]
   55
```

32)
```
  [  ]
+  34
   71
```

33)
```
   28
+ [  ]
   60
```

34)
```
  [  ]
+  15
   38
```

35)
```
   23
+ [  ]
   34
```

36)
```
  [  ]
+  30
   44
```

37)
```
   37
+ [  ]
   62
```

38)
```
  [  ]
+  10
   24
```

39)
```
   21
+ [  ]
   41
```

40)
```
  [  ]
+  34
   60
```

41)
```
   22
+ [  ]
   35
```

42)
```
  [  ]
+  14
   24
```

43)
```
   18
+ [  ]
   31
```

44)
```
  [  ]
+  28
   46
```

45)
```
   16
+ [  ]
   28
```

46)
```
  [  ]
+  20
   53
```

47)
```
   10
+ [  ]
   23
```

48)
```
  [  ]
+  31
   52
```

49)
```
   24
+ [  ]
   56
```

50)
```
  [  ]
+  19
   30
```

51)
```
   10
+ [  ]
   46
```

52)
```
  [  ]
+  40
   64
```

53)
```
   19
+ [  ]
   33
```

54)
```
  [  ]
+  28
   63
```

55)
```
   27
+ [  ]
   66
```

56)
```
  [  ]
+  14
   32
```

57)
```
   15
+ [  ]
   36
```

58)
```
  [  ]
+  26
   51
```

59)
```
   37
+ [  ]
   57
```

60)
```
  [  ]
+  22
   42
```

1) 31 + ☐ = 60

2) ☐ + 29 = 66

3) 28 + ☐ = 40

4) ☐ + 14 = 50

5) 26 + ☐ = 60

6) ☐ + 22 = 45

7) 36 + ☐ = 71

8) ☐ + 22 = 45

9) 25 + ☐ = 53

10) ☐ + 11 = 43

11) 40 + ☐ = 72

12) ☐ + 35 = 58

13) 38 + ☐ = 63

14) ☐ + 36 = 54

15) 32 + ☐ = 69

16) ☐ + 20 = 59

17) 10 + ☐ = 47

18) ☐ + 36 = 64

19) 34 + ☐ = 51

20) ☐ + 33 = 67

21) 27 + ☐ = 54

22) ☐ + 25 = 55

23) 13 + ☐ = 26

24) ☐ + 20 = 44

25) 24 + ☐ = 36

26) ☐ + 12 = 33

27) 33 + ☐ = 45

28) ☐ + 31 = 62

29) 10 + ☐ = 22

30) ☐ + 37 = 64

31) 31 + ☐ = 61

32) ☐ + 39 = 49

33) 20 + ☐ = 59

34) ☐ + 18 = 48

35) 40 + ☐ = 75

36) ☐ + 17 = 57

37) 40 + ☐ = 54

38) ☐ + 35 = 73

39) 19 + ☐ = 40

40) ☐ + 11 = 29

41) 10 + ☐ = 20

42) ☐ + 17 = 41

43) 35 + ☐ = 74

44) ☐ + 31 = 59

45) 18 + ☐ = 47

46) ☐ + 31 = 53

47) 37 + ☐ = 55

48) ☐ + 35 = 64

49) 21 + ☐ = 43

50) ☐ + 18 = 36

51) 20 + ☐ = 38

52) ☐ + 40 = 78

53) 36 + ☐ = 47

54) ☐ + 30 = 49

55) 35 + ☐ = 55

56) ☐ + 23 = 45

57) 38 + ☐ = 59

58) ☐ + 35 = 53

59) 10 + ☐ = 38

60) ☐ + 36 = 49

1) 39 + □ = 57

2) □ + 37 = 70

3) 15 + □ = 33

4) □ + 25 = 43

5) 26 + □ = 46

6) □ + 22 = 57

7) 34 + □ = 56

8) □ + 28 = 58

9) 40 + □ = 78

10) □ + 20 = 30

11) 12 + □ = 25

12) □ + 24 = 58

13) 33 + □ = 65

14) □ + 13 = 41

15) 33 + □ = 53

16) □ + 37 = 49

17) 14 + □ = 43

18) □ + 23 = 53

19) 31 + □ = 45

20) □ + 12 = 41

21) 15 + □ = 45

22) □ + 20 = 54

23) 14 + □ = 25

24) □ + 10 = 42

25) 29 + □ = 64

26) □ + 40 = 52

27) 31 + □ = 54

28) □ + 17 = 29

29) 30 + □ = 61

30) □ + 35 = 57

31) 17 + □ = 48

32) □ + 16 = 35

33) 18 + □ = 35

34) □ + 20 = 52

35) 35 + □ = 73

36) □ + 28 = 56

37) 39 + □ = 51

38) □ + 32 = 64

39) 40 + □ = 70

40) □ + 21 = 43

41) 39 + □ = 50

42) □ + 32 = 65

43) 11 + □ = 31

44) □ + 17 = 45

45) 30 + □ = 64

46) □ + 40 = 70

47) 27 + □ = 59

48) □ + 35 = 73

49) 40 + □ = 53

50) □ + 23 = 63

51) 39 + □ = 61

52) □ + 16 = 42

53) 36 + □ = 70

54) □ + 11 = 42

55) 26 + □ = 64

56) □ + 12 = 37

57) 30 + □ = 41

58) □ + 29 = 39

59) 40 + □ = 55

60) □ + 36 = 46

1) $29 + \boxed{} = 68$	2) $\boxed{} + 30 = 70$	3) $29 + \boxed{} = 48$	4) $\boxed{} + 32 = 48$	5) $12 + \boxed{} = 44$	6) $\boxed{} + 23 = 45$
7) $40 + \boxed{} = 55$	8) $\boxed{} + 36 = 58$	9) $29 + \boxed{} = 41$	10) $\boxed{} + 33 = 44$	11) $26 + \boxed{} = 63$	12) $\boxed{} + 40 = 58$
13) $37 + \boxed{} = 77$	14) $\boxed{} + 17 = 44$	15) $23 + \boxed{} = 60$	16) $\boxed{} + 24 = 44$	17) $37 + \boxed{} = 53$	18) $\boxed{} + 35 = 65$
19) $34 + \boxed{} = 63$	20) $\boxed{} + 17 = 54$	21) $40 + \boxed{} = 80$	22) $\boxed{} + 33 = 57$	23) $14 + \boxed{} = 38$	24) $\boxed{} + 21 = 34$
25) $19 + \boxed{} = 43$	26) $\boxed{} + 38 = 48$	27) $16 + \boxed{} = 55$	28) $\boxed{} + 17 = 39$	29) $20 + \boxed{} = 56$	30) $\boxed{} + 12 = 39$
31) $31 + \boxed{} = 42$	32) $\boxed{} + 12 = 22$	33) $37 + \boxed{} = 55$	34) $\boxed{} + 14 = 49$	35) $26 + \boxed{} = 49$	36) $\boxed{} + 28 = 50$
37) $21 + \boxed{} = 37$	38) $\boxed{} + 11 = 24$	39) $39 + \boxed{} = 54$	40) $\boxed{} + 30 = 42$	41) $20 + \boxed{} = 58$	42) $\boxed{} + 21 = 41$
43) $11 + \boxed{} = 42$	44) $\boxed{} + 18 = 44$	45) $31 + \boxed{} = 54$	46) $\boxed{} + 18 = 41$	47) $21 + \boxed{} = 59$	48) $\boxed{} + 10 = 34$
49) $22 + \boxed{} = 34$	50) $\boxed{} + 13 = 23$	51) $18 + \boxed{} = 45$	52) $\boxed{} + 27 = 58$	53) $37 + \boxed{} = 77$	54) $\boxed{} + 15 = 45$
55) $24 + \boxed{} = 51$	56) $\boxed{} + 32 = 60$	57) $28 + \boxed{} = 58$	58) $\boxed{} + 15 = 44$	59) $25 + \boxed{} = 64$	60) $\boxed{} + 27 = 61$

1) 38 + ☐ = 65

2) ☐ + 20 = 53

3) 32 + ☐ = 72

4) ☐ + 19 = 59

5) 26 + ☐ = 45

6) ☐ + 24 = 64

7) 23 + ☐ = 47

8) ☐ + 14 = 33

9) 32 + ☐ = 47

10) ☐ + 19 = 53

11) 18 + ☐ = 46

12) ☐ + 27 = 38

13) 35 + ☐ = 65

14) ☐ + 36 = 55

15) 30 + ☐ = 41

16) ☐ + 12 = 27

17) 24 + ☐ = 56

18) ☐ + 11 = 27

19) 39 + ☐ = 72

20) ☐ + 30 = 47

21) 20 + ☐ = 41

22) ☐ + 32 = 55

23) 37 + ☐ = 49

24) ☐ + 31 = 43

25) 39 + ☐ = 61

26) ☐ + 34 = 54

27) 11 + ☐ = 28

28) ☐ + 22 = 62

29) 18 + ☐ = 28

30) ☐ + 11 = 32

31) 21 + ☐ = 51

32) ☐ + 32 = 63

33) 11 + ☐ = 51

34) ☐ + 13 = 26

35) 26 + ☐ = 59

36) ☐ + 29 = 40

37) 15 + ☐ = 35

38) ☐ + 22 = 51

39) 24 + ☐ = 47

40) ☐ + 34 = 70

41) 20 + ☐ = 42

42) ☐ + 22 = 37

43) 15 + ☐ = 32

44) ☐ + 12 = 52

45) 15 + ☐ = 43

46) ☐ + 37 = 67

47) 24 + ☐ = 39

48) ☐ + 37 = 57

49) 38 + ☐ = 74

50) ☐ + 25 = 64

51) 14 + ☐ = 51

52) ☐ + 21 = 46

53) 35 + ☐ = 46

54) ☐ + 20 = 59

55) 24 + ☐ = 63

56) ☐ + 21 = 37

57) 22 + ☐ = 33

58) ☐ + 22 = 36

59) 33 + ☐ = 63

60) ☐ + 37 = 68

1) 44 + 63

2) 44 + 42

3) 63 + 65

4) 59 + 69

5) 53 + 64

6) 60 + 49

7) 69 + 55

8) 56 + 68

9) 42 + 44

10) 67 + 69

11) 55 + 51

12) 67 + 60

13) 66 + 67

14) 59 + 64

15) 56 + 59

16) 54 + 49

17) 64 + 58

18) 65 + 56

19) 57 + 61

20) 42 + 63

21) 58 + 51

22) 50 + 63

23) 61 + 47

24) 68 + 57

25) 44 + 56

26) 45 + 57

27) 70 + 66

28) 44 + 69

29) 70 + 68

30) 53 + 54

31) 63 + 47

32) 43 + 70

33) 66 + 69

34) 70 + 57

35) 48 + 49

36) 51 + 44

37) 42 + 42

38) 56 + 50

39) 53 + 53

40) 48 + 58

41) 51 + 40

42) 54 + 61

43) 60 + 49

44) 70 + 69

45) 53 + 48

46) 46 + 68

47) 63 + 50

48) 68 + 48

49) 51 + 67

50) 41 + 50

51) 59 + 57

52) 52 + 52

53) 69 + 67

54) 55 + 41

55) 66 + 64

56) 40 + 57

57) 40 + 50

58) 54 + 55

59) 45 + 41

60) 54 + 65

1)   43
  + 63

2)   48
  + 40

3)   65
  + 59

4)   68
  + 47

5)   70
  + 46

6)   67
  + 62

7)   55
  + 55

8)   50
  + 66

9)   70
  + 61

10)   48
  + 47

11)   67
  + 40

12)   65
  + 46

13)   56
  + 68

14)   49
  + 65

15)   48
  + 50

16)   49
  + 70

17)   40
  + 45

18)   61
  + 49

19)   56
  + 44

20)   61
  + 53

21)   61
  + 61

22)   57
  + 61

23)   55
  + 48

24)   57
  + 64

25)   60
  + 46

26)   45
  + 67

27)   61
  + 46

28)   69
  + 68

29)   42
  + 54

30)   41
  + 40

31)   69
  + 42

32)   47
  + 49

33)   57
  + 50

34)   54
  + 70

35)   40
  + 57

36)   67
  + 53

37)   41
  + 44

38)   42
  + 62

39)   68
  + 67

40)   69
  + 66

41)   63
  + 53

42)   63
  + 50

43)   63
  + 40

44)   43
  + 47

45)   60
  + 69

46)   65
  + 56

47)   49
  + 51

48)   59
  + 64

49)   49
  + 46

50)   40
  + 57

51)   62
  + 51

52)   62
  + 70

53)   44
  + 56

54)   68
  + 59

55)   40
  + 56

56)   67
  + 70

57)   40
  + 45

58)   70
  + 67

59)   65
  + 48

60)   69
  + 66

1) 53 + 49

2) 51 + 60

3) 62 + 68

4) 57 + 55

5) 65 + 63

6) 41 + 48

7) 53 + 58

8) 68 + 47

9) 70 + 43

10) 57 + 56

11) 51 + 50

12) 60 + 63

13) 54 + 41

14) 51 + 52

15) 56 + 69

16) 66 + 42

17) 40 + 68

18) 43 + 61

19) 69 + 41

20) 58 + 65

21) 57 + 62

22) 41 + 58

23) 45 + 48

24) 64 + 60

25) 48 + 58

26) 63 + 40

27) 53 + 65

28) 57 + 48

29) 56 + 54

30) 57 + 61

31) 64 + 54

32) 58 + 49

33) 43 + 45

34) 54 + 56

35) 40 + 65

36) 67 + 69

37) 53 + 49

38) 50 + 53

39) 60 + 65

40) 69 + 48

41) 61 + 59

42) 64 + 66

43) 51 + 41

44) 58 + 66

45) 52 + 56

46) 67 + 54

47) 58 + 64

48) 40 + 63

49) 58 + 57

50) 70 + 45

51) 70 + 44

52) 70 + 54

53) 47 + 43

54) 48 + 49

55) 68 + 67

56) 69 + 59

57) 68 + 56

58) 58 + 44

59) 48 + 56

60) 69 + 55

Time: | Name:

1) 48 + 43

2) 49 + 41

3) 66 + 61

4) 59 + 54

5) 49 + 51

6) 53 + 44

7) 42 + 47

8) 62 + 69

9) 61 + 48

10) 69 + 60

11) 44 + 49

12) 55 + 41

13) 68 + 41

14) 59 + 49

15) 49 + 52

16) 53 + 49

17) 52 + 52

18) 54 + 41

19) 55 + 56

20) 57 + 53

21) 53 + 49

22) 46 + 63

23) 64 + 45

24) 56 + 50

25) 68 + 48

26) 46 + 51

27) 62 + 67

28) 43 + 68

29) 44 + 49

30) 66 + 41

31) 58 + 61

32) 49 + 50

33) 54 + 52

34) 66 + 65

35) 40 + 70

36) 70 + 42

37) 49 + 46

38) 64 + 40

39) 69 + 69

40) 50 + 52

41) 61 + 60

42) 57 + 40

43) 55 + 45

44) 62 + 41

45) 51 + 62

46) 59 + 66

47) 45 + 65

48) 65 + 40

49) 45 + 59

50) 64 + 50

51) 70 + 59

52) 57 + 62

53) 64 + 60

54) 45 + 56

55) 54 + 60

56) 41 + 56

57) 50 + 48

58) 50 + 48

59) 51 + 49

60) 54 + 69

1) 52 + 64

2) 58 + 66

3) 65 + 43

4) 60 + 63

5) 52 + 58

6) 44 + 58

7) 63 + 54

8) 52 + 52

9) 51 + 57

10) 66 + 62

11) 67 + 56

12) 44 + 53

13) 63 + 41

14) 69 + 47

15) 52 + 63

16) 62 + 48

17) 64 + 65

18) 43 + 60

19) 61 + 70

20) 69 + 56

21) 45 + 69

22) 49 + 49

23) 41 + 44

24) 70 + 55

25) 55 + 45

26) 45 + 40

27) 61 + 67

28) 57 + 50

29) 61 + 58

30) 57 + 44

31) 52 + 45

32) 40 + 57

33) 42 + 49

34) 44 + 45

35) 45 + 56

36) 59 + 59

37) 43 + 41

38) 55 + 67

39) 68 + 55

40) 46 + 65

41) 62 + 61

42) 58 + 43

43) 53 + 53

44) 59 + 45

45) 59 + 56

46) 42 + 44

47) 65 + 57

48) 56 + 43

49) 59 + 46

50) 64 + 65

51) 43 + 50

52) 53 + 64

53) 40 + 41

54) 63 + 50

55) 43 + 68

56) 54 + 67

57) 41 + 56

58) 61 + 40

59) 50 + 69

60) 52 + 57

1) 58 + ☐ = 112

2) ☐ + 43 = 85

3) 47 + ☐ = 91

4) ☐ + 47 = 113

5) 47 + ☐ = 109

6) ☐ + 45 = 107

7) 41 + ☐ = 104

8) ☐ + 47 = 102

9) 47 + ☐ = 115

10) ☐ + 40 = 106

11) 47 + ☐ = 110

12) ☐ + 68 = 133

13) 41 + ☐ = 85

14) ☐ + 46 = 103

15) 54 + ☐ = 98

16) ☐ + 57 = 116

17) 61 + ☐ = 107

18) ☐ + 60 = 128

19) 53 + ☐ = 102

20) ☐ + 52 = 94

21) 57 + ☐ = 104

22) ☐ + 54 = 114

23) 52 + ☐ = 106

24) ☐ + 53 = 122

25) 46 + ☐ = 113

26) ☐ + 62 = 125

27) 44 + ☐ = 90

28) ☐ + 56 = 113

29) 68 + ☐ = 129

30) ☐ + 60 = 124

31) 56 + ☐ = 115

32) ☐ + 61 = 125

33) 60 + ☐ = 106

34) ☐ + 42 = 111

35) 60 + ☐ = 120

36) ☐ + 51 = 92

37) 61 + ☐ = 109

38) ☐ + 53 = 104

39) 58 + ☐ = 126

40) ☐ + 59 = 121

41) 67 + ☐ = 128

42) ☐ + 56 = 112

43) 65 + ☐ = 106

44) ☐ + 42 = 105

45) 62 + ☐ = 111

46) ☐ + 60 = 104

47) 63 + ☐ = 116

48) ☐ + 61 = 131

49) 56 + ☐ = 99

50) ☐ + 55 = 115

51) 47 + ☐ = 108

52) ☐ + 62 = 107

53) 48 + ☐ = 114

54) ☐ + 65 = 109

55) 46 + ☐ = 88

56) ☐ + 45 = 98

57) 45 + ☐ = 95

58) ☐ + 68 = 113

59) 70 + ☐ = 133

60) ☐ + 47 = 96

1) 43 + ☐ = 88

2) ☐ + 62 = 112

3) 54 + ☐ = 99

4) ☐ + 49 = 95

5) 52 + ☐ = 108

6) ☐ + 52 = 92

7) 46 + ☐ = 113

8) ☐ + 68 = 134

9) 67 + ☐ = 123

10) ☐ + 52 = 109

11) 46 + ☐ = 94

12) ☐ + 67 = 129

13) 40 + ☐ = 96

14) ☐ + 44 = 111

15) 49 + ☐ = 108

16) ☐ + 64 = 117

17) 64 + ☐ = 114

18) ☐ + 43 = 90

19) 66 + ☐ = 118

20) ☐ + 47 = 117

21) 50 + ☐ = 95

22) ☐ + 51 = 118

23) 62 + ☐ = 121

24) ☐ + 59 = 119

25) 67 + ☐ = 134

26) ☐ + 61 = 120

27) 56 + ☐ = 104

28) ☐ + 60 = 114

29) 53 + ☐ = 115

30) ☐ + 40 = 94

31) 68 + ☐ = 115

32) ☐ + 57 = 120

33) 44 + ☐ = 90

34) ☐ + 46 = 97

35) 56 + ☐ = 118

36) ☐ + 57 = 118

37) 43 + ☐ = 89

38) ☐ + 55 = 104

39) 50 + ☐ = 92

40) ☐ + 53 = 97

41) 50 + ☐ = 113

42) ☐ + 58 = 111

43) 60 + ☐ = 107

44) ☐ + 47 = 107

45) 63 + ☐ = 113

46) ☐ + 60 = 102

47) 56 + ☐ = 125

48) ☐ + 56 = 117

49) 62 + ☐ = 125

50) ☐ + 51 = 95

51) 48 + ☐ = 94

52) ☐ + 56 = 103

53) 43 + ☐ = 89

54) ☐ + 65 = 106

55) 40 + ☐ = 85

56) ☐ + 63 = 107

57) 43 + ☐ = 88

58) ☐ + 44 = 108

59) 69 + ☐ = 138

60) ☐ + 57 = 110

1) 41
  + ☐
  83

2) ☐
  + 52
  115

3) 66
  + ☐
  118

4) ☐
  + 53
  107

5) 40
  + ☐
  84

6) ☐
  + 51
  91

7) 62
  + ☐
  106

8) ☐
  + 59
  116

9) 56
  + ☐
  99

10) ☐
  + 60
  113

11) 66
  + ☐
  118

12) ☐
  + 42
  91

13) 65
  + ☐
  109

14) ☐
  + 62
  129

15) 60
  + ☐
  121

16) ☐
  + 54
  112

17) 44
  + ☐
  108

18) ☐
  + 63
  124

19) 62
  + ☐
  125

20) ☐
  + 63
  123

21) 58
  + ☐
  98

22) ☐
  + 67
  136

23) 61
  + ☐
  130

24) ☐
  + 56
  104

25) 47
  + ☐
  88

26) ☐
  + 49
  110

27) 57
  + ☐
  110

28) ☐
  + 52
  96

29) 64
  + ☐
  134

30) ☐
  + 68
  119

31) 48
  + ☐
  93

32) ☐
  + 67
  110

33) 44
  + ☐
  96

34) ☐
  + 61
  124

35) 54
  + ☐
  113

36) ☐
  + 51
  99

37) 59
  + ☐
  105

38) ☐
  + 45
  98

39) 45
  + ☐
  97

40) ☐
  + 59
  112

41) 69
  + ☐
  134

42) ☐
  + 46
  99

43) 64
  + ☐
  110

44) ☐
  + 51
  93

45) 45
  + ☐
  89

46) ☐
  + 44
  94

47) 44
  + ☐
  92

48) ☐
  + 46
  86

49) 55
  + ☐
  122

50) ☐
  + 43
  84

51) 70
  + ☐
  126

52) ☐
  + 41
  94

53) 70
  + ☐
  111

54) ☐
  + 52
  95

55) 56
  + ☐
  101

56) ☐
  + 47
  87

57) 42
  + ☐
  110

58) ☐
  + 57
  110

59) 57
  + ☐
  102

60) ☐
  + 61
  113

1)
$$\begin{array}{r} 60 \\ + \boxed{} \\ \hline 106 \end{array}$$

2)
$$\begin{array}{r} \boxed{} \\ + 54 \\ \hline 122 \end{array}$$

3)
$$\begin{array}{r} 49 \\ + \boxed{} \\ \hline 113 \end{array}$$

4)
$$\begin{array}{r} \boxed{} \\ + 55 \\ \hline 102 \end{array}$$

5)
$$\begin{array}{r} 68 \\ + \boxed{} \\ \hline 115 \end{array}$$

6)
$$\begin{array}{r} \boxed{} \\ + 47 \\ \hline 102 \end{array}$$

7)
$$\begin{array}{r} 45 \\ + \boxed{} \\ \hline 106 \end{array}$$

8)
$$\begin{array}{r} \boxed{} \\ + 46 \\ \hline 106 \end{array}$$

9)
$$\begin{array}{r} 54 \\ + \boxed{} \\ \hline 96 \end{array}$$

10)
$$\begin{array}{r} \boxed{} \\ + 42 \\ \hline 112 \end{array}$$

11)
$$\begin{array}{r} 70 \\ + \boxed{} \\ \hline 110 \end{array}$$

12)
$$\begin{array}{r} \boxed{} \\ + 53 \\ \hline 115 \end{array}$$

13)
$$\begin{array}{r} 53 \\ + \boxed{} \\ \hline 93 \end{array}$$

14)
$$\begin{array}{r} \boxed{} \\ + 64 \\ \hline 111 \end{array}$$

15)
$$\begin{array}{r} 43 \\ + \boxed{} \\ \hline 89 \end{array}$$

16)
$$\begin{array}{r} \boxed{} \\ + 70 \\ \hline 117 \end{array}$$

17)
$$\begin{array}{r} 45 \\ + \boxed{} \\ \hline 98 \end{array}$$

18)
$$\begin{array}{r} \boxed{} \\ + 66 \\ \hline 128 \end{array}$$

19)
$$\begin{array}{r} 70 \\ + \boxed{} \\ \hline 136 \end{array}$$

20)
$$\begin{array}{r} \boxed{} \\ + 55 \\ \hline 98 \end{array}$$

21)
$$\begin{array}{r} 53 \\ + \boxed{} \\ \hline 105 \end{array}$$

22)
$$\begin{array}{r} \boxed{} \\ + 48 \\ \hline 93 \end{array}$$

23)
$$\begin{array}{r} 48 \\ + \boxed{} \\ \hline 117 \end{array}$$

24)
$$\begin{array}{r} \boxed{} \\ + 45 \\ \hline 94 \end{array}$$

25)
$$\begin{array}{r} 53 \\ + \boxed{} \\ \hline 114 \end{array}$$

26)
$$\begin{array}{r} \boxed{} \\ + 50 \\ \hline 98 \end{array}$$

27)
$$\begin{array}{r} 40 \\ + \boxed{} \\ \hline 104 \end{array}$$

28)
$$\begin{array}{r} \boxed{} \\ + 62 \\ \hline 117 \end{array}$$

29)
$$\begin{array}{r} 43 \\ + \boxed{} \\ \hline 104 \end{array}$$

30)
$$\begin{array}{r} \boxed{} \\ + 43 \\ \hline 87 \end{array}$$

31)
$$\begin{array}{r} 43 \\ + \boxed{} \\ \hline 90 \end{array}$$

32)
$$\begin{array}{r} \boxed{} \\ + 61 \\ \hline 109 \end{array}$$

33)
$$\begin{array}{r} 52 \\ + \boxed{} \\ \hline 109 \end{array}$$

34)
$$\begin{array}{r} \boxed{} \\ + 54 \\ \hline 95 \end{array}$$

35)
$$\begin{array}{r} 64 \\ + \boxed{} \\ \hline 105 \end{array}$$

36)
$$\begin{array}{r} \boxed{} \\ + 52 \\ \hline 106 \end{array}$$

37)
$$\begin{array}{r} 49 \\ + \boxed{} \\ \hline 103 \end{array}$$

38)
$$\begin{array}{r} \boxed{} \\ + 51 \\ \hline 102 \end{array}$$

39)
$$\begin{array}{r} 68 \\ + \boxed{} \\ \hline 125 \end{array}$$

40)
$$\begin{array}{r} \boxed{} \\ + 41 \\ \hline 103 \end{array}$$

41)
$$\begin{array}{r} 50 \\ + \boxed{} \\ \hline 116 \end{array}$$

42)
$$\begin{array}{r} \boxed{} \\ + 43 \\ \hline 100 \end{array}$$

43)
$$\begin{array}{r} 45 \\ + \boxed{} \\ \hline 105 \end{array}$$

44)
$$\begin{array}{r} \boxed{} \\ + 46 \\ \hline 107 \end{array}$$

45)
$$\begin{array}{r} 66 \\ + \boxed{} \\ \hline 118 \end{array}$$

46)
$$\begin{array}{r} \boxed{} \\ + 59 \\ \hline 120 \end{array}$$

47)
$$\begin{array}{r} 51 \\ + \boxed{} \\ \hline 117 \end{array}$$

48)
$$\begin{array}{r} \boxed{} \\ + 43 \\ \hline 110 \end{array}$$

49)
$$\begin{array}{r} 65 \\ + \boxed{} \\ \hline 120 \end{array}$$

50)
$$\begin{array}{r} \boxed{} \\ + 53 \\ \hline 113 \end{array}$$

51)
$$\begin{array}{r} 47 \\ + \boxed{} \\ \hline 115 \end{array}$$

52)
$$\begin{array}{r} \boxed{} \\ + 58 \\ \hline 108 \end{array}$$

53)
$$\begin{array}{r} 42 \\ + \boxed{} \\ \hline 109 \end{array}$$

54)
$$\begin{array}{r} \boxed{} \\ + 55 \\ \hline 119 \end{array}$$

55)
$$\begin{array}{r} 56 \\ + \boxed{} \\ \hline 125 \end{array}$$

56)
$$\begin{array}{r} \boxed{} \\ + 41 \\ \hline 107 \end{array}$$

57)
$$\begin{array}{r} 60 \\ + \boxed{} \\ \hline 127 \end{array}$$

58)
$$\begin{array}{r} \boxed{} \\ + 46 \\ \hline 91 \end{array}$$

59)
$$\begin{array}{r} 53 \\ + \boxed{} \\ \hline 103 \end{array}$$

60)
$$\begin{array}{r} \boxed{} \\ + 55 \\ \hline 125 \end{array}$$

1) 43 + ☐ = 87

2) ☐ + 63 = 107

3) 47 + ☐ = 98

4) ☐ + 69 = 126

5) 69 + ☐ = 136

6) ☐ + 40 = 84

7) 70 + ☐ = 112

8) ☐ + 55 = 99

9) 61 + ☐ = 107

10) ☐ + 42 = 84

11) 55 + ☐ = 119

12) ☐ + 65 = 119

13) 69 + ☐ = 125

14) ☐ + 54 = 105

15) 50 + ☐ = 112

16) ☐ + 52 = 105

17) 42 + ☐ = 89

18) ☐ + 68 = 112

19) 51 + ☐ = 96

20) ☐ + 59 = 111

21) 62 + ☐ = 112

22) ☐ + 46 = 101

23) 56 + ☐ = 106

24) ☐ + 69 = 118

25) 67 + ☐ = 115

26) ☐ + 70 = 140

27) 42 + ☐ = 111

28) ☐ + 54 = 108

29) 69 + ☐ = 117

30) ☐ + 40 = 105

31) 64 + ☐ = 106

32) ☐ + 60 = 123

33) 45 + ☐ = 100

34) ☐ + 41 = 104

35) 61 + ☐ = 111

36) ☐ + 66 = 123

37) 40 + ☐ = 84

38) ☐ + 44 = 99

39) 64 + ☐ = 118

40) ☐ + 63 = 118

41) 44 + ☐ = 97

42) ☐ + 55 = 120

43) 50 + ☐ = 92

44) ☐ + 69 = 110

45) 66 + ☐ = 121

46) ☐ + 52 = 94

47) 49 + ☐ = 113

48) ☐ + 46 = 109

49) 56 + ☐ = 114

50) ☐ + 53 = 112

51) 55 + ☐ = 109

52) ☐ + 66 = 129

53) 56 + ☐ = 114

54) ☐ + 70 = 123

55) 41 + ☐ = 98

56) ☐ + 44 = 96

57) 41 + ☐ = 99

58) ☐ + 64 = 122

59) 56 + ☐ = 121

60) ☐ + 50 = 113

1) 76 + 99

2) 96 + 86

3) 75 + 100

4) 92 + 95

5) 87 + 79

6) 99 + 85

7) 71 + 74

8) 94 + 74

9) 73 + 88

10) 73 + 82

11) 71 + 73

12) 87 + 93

13) 78 + 95

14) 72 + 81

15) 83 + 73

16) 93 + 79

17) 81 + 92

18) 95 + 90

19) 86 + 97

20) 82 + 92

21) 78 + 86

22) 100 + 72

23) 99 + 93

24) 99 + 95

25) 89 + 95

26) 72 + 76

27) 90 + 78

28) 95 + 90

29) 73 + 85

30) 73 + 88

31) 71 + 94

32) 73 + 81

33) 98 + 78

34) 89 + 71

35) 99 + 94

36) 73 + 79

37) 77 + 70

38) 80 + 91

39) 71 + 77

40) 71 + 80

41) 75 + 100

42) 95 + 81

43) 81 + 70

44) 94 + 74

45) 71 + 98

46) 78 + 77

47) 99 + 70

48) 94 + 94

49) 79 + 92

50) 86 + 87

51) 86 + 75

52) 76 + 99

53) 77 + 98

54) 75 + 85

55) 99 + 79

56) 95 + 70

57) 73 + 93

58) 86 + 82

59) 83 + 91

60) 72 + 89

1) 70 + 89

2) 70 + 98

3) 70 + 77

4) 70 + 74

5) 70 + 72

6) 70 + 83

7) 70 + 91

8) 70 + 87

9) 70 + 92

10) 70 + 76

11) 70 + 73

12) 70 + 88

13) 70 + 74

14) 70 + 70

15) 70 + 99

16) 70 + 94

17) 70 + 80

18) 70 + 95

19) 70 + 74

20) 70 + 84

21) 70 + 94

22) 70 + 93

23) 70 + 99

24) 70 + 84

25) 70 + 93

26) 70 + 94

27) 70 + 73

28) 70 + 90

29) 70 + 98

30) 70 + 92

31) 70 + 73

32) 70 + 78

33) 70 + 72

34) 70 + 86

35) 70 + 96

36) 70 + 98

37) 70 + 89

38) 70 + 88

39) 70 + 73

40) 70 + 79

41) 70 + 82

42) 70 + 72

43) 70 + 76

44) 70 + 94

45) 70 + 91

46) 70 + 100

47) 70 + 96

48) 70 + 99

49) 70 + 83

50) 70 + 98

51) 70 + 74

52) 70 + 79

53) 70 + 98

54) 70 + 70

55) 70 + 96

56) 70 + 92

57) 70 + 98

58) 70 + 90

59) 70 + 100

60) 70 + 95

1)
```
   92
+  90
```
2)
```
   89
+  90
```
3)
```
   78
+  81
```
4)
```
   77
+  92
```
5)
```
   89
+  96
```
6)
```
   79
+  98
```

7)
```
   76
+  77
```
8)
```
   85
+  85
```
9)
```
   79
+  89
```
10)
```
  100
+  72
```
11)
```
   88
+  84
```
12)
```
   77
+  86
```

13)
```
   88
+  82
```
14)
```
   92
+  74
```
15)
```
   86
+  91
```
16)
```
   86
+  76
```
17)
```
   78
+  93
```
18)
```
   75
+  90
```

19)
```
   85
+  73
```
20)
```
   72
+  76
```
21)
```
  100
+  95
```
22)
```
   79
+  90
```
23)
```
   70
+  85
```
24)
```
   86
+  83
```

25)
```
   74
+  91
```
26)
```
   95
+  74
```
27)
```
   70
+  85
```
28)
```
   70
+  83
```
29)
```
   76
+  93
```
30)
```
   85
+  71
```

31)
```
   83
+  80
```
32)
```
   82
+  76
```
33)
```
   79
+  92
```
34)
```
   97
+  73
```
35)
```
   71
+  73
```
36)
```
   71
+  80
```

37)
```
   99
+  83
```
38)
```
   82
+  84
```
39)
```
   99
+  76
```
40)
```
   73
+  86
```
41)
```
   99
+  92
```
42)
```
   97
+  86
```

43)
```
   77
+  75
```
44)
```
   82
+  71
```
45)
```
   93
+  93
```
46)
```
  100
+ 100
```
47)
```
   74
+  84
```
48)
```
   72
+  87
```

49)
```
   91
+  97
```
50)
```
   85
+  77
```
51)
```
   75
+  73
```
52)
```
   88
+  78
```
53)
```
   83
+  72
```
54)
```
   73
+  82
```

55)
```
   80
+  77
```
56)
```
  100
+  70
```
57)
```
   98
+  96
```
58)
```
   85
+  71
```
59)
```
   70
+  70
```
60)
```
   72
+  99
```

1) 100
  + 93

2) 77
  + 92

3) 73
  + 74

4) 88
  + 81

5) 94
  + 85

6) 85
  + 77

7) 78
  + 80

8) 88
  + 98

9) 93
  + 92

10) 74
  + 98

11) 93
  + 100

12) 97
  + 79

13) 86
  + 75

14) 80
  + 98

15) 79
  + 83

16) 80
  + 81

17) 82
  + 94

18) 72
  + 77

19) 91
  + 100

20) 70
  + 70

21) 89
  + 100

22) 87
  + 87

23) 77
  + 73

24) 82
  + 86

25) 72
  + 92

26) 80
  + 78

27) 95
  + 85

28) 86
  + 96

29) 91
  + 82

30) 97
  + 80

31) 93
  + 78

32) 92
  + 86

33) 71
  + 91

34) 87
  + 98

35) 75
  + 92

36) 72
  + 91

37) 86
  + 88

38) 93
  + 86

39) 80
  + 88

40) 93
  + 90

41) 83
  + 97

42) 78
  + 70

43) 80
  + 80

44) 98
  + 80

45) 77
  + 72

46) 73
  + 100

47) 70
  + 87

48) 82
  + 73

49) 88
  + 76

50) 97
  + 88

51) 96
  + 82

52) 91
  + 71

53) 84
  + 83

54) 96
  + 86

55) 77
  + 70

56) 82
  + 73

57) 100
  + 80

58) 84
  + 100

59) 74
  + 81

60) 91
  + 97

1) 98 + 88

2) 83 + 96

3) 92 + 82

4) 93 + 77

5) 82 + 87

6) 89 + 98

7) 85 + 92

8) 98 + 88

9) 79 + 85

10) 72 + 78

11) 84 + 78

12) 76 + 89

13) 77 + 99

14) 99 + 70

15) 85 + 71

16) 83 + 85

17) 74 + 99

18) 76 + 78

19) 87 + 84

20) 86 + 86

21) 71 + 94

22) 99 + 82

23) 83 + 79

24) 78 + 84

25) 80 + 87

26) 85 + 87

27) 90 + 82

28) 100 + 100

29) 76 + 73

30) 82 + 84

31) 70 + 90

32) 71 + 81

33) 78 + 85

34) 79 + 91

35) 88 + 75

36) 80 + 91

37) 77 + 79

38) 78 + 89

39) 84 + 76

40) 97 + 96

41) 96 + 86

42) 91 + 99

43) 89 + 77

44) 93 + 91

45) 87 + 83

46) 76 + 91

47) 94 + 96

48) 85 + 74

49) 91 + 77

50) 83 + 81

51) 100 + 87

52) 95 + 89

53) 76 + 98

54) 80 + 79

55) 84 + 99

56) 71 + 100

57) 70 + 87

58) 79 + 76

59) 77 + 97

60) 100 + 84

1)
```
   81
+ [ ]
 161
```

2)
```
 [ ]
+ 70
 170
```

3)
```
   89
+ [ ]
 182
```

4)
```
 [ ]
+ 84
 157
```

5)
```
   73
+ [ ]
 147
```

6)
```
 [ ]
+ 83
 169
```

7)
```
   93
+ [ ]
 188
```

8)
```
 [ ]
+ 78
 162
```

9)
```
   75
+ [ ]
 168
```

10)
```
 [ ]
+ 70
 156
```

11)
```
   87
+ [ ]
 169
```

12)
```
 [ ]
+ 88
 172
```

13)
```
   98
+ [ ]
 197
```

14)
```
 [ ]
+ 74
 155
```

15)
```
   73
+ [ ]
 156
```

16)
```
 [ ]
+ 93
 183
```

17)
```
   94
+ [ ]
 192
```

18)
```
 [ ]
+ 85
 164
```

19)
```
   96
+ [ ]
 189
```

20)
```
 [ ]
+ 97
 190
```

21)
```
   99
+ [ ]
 184
```

22)
```
 [ ]
+ 95
 190
```

23)
```
   90
+ [ ]
 166
```

24)
```
 [ ]
+ 82
 182
```

25)
```
  100
+ [ ]
 180
```

26)
```
 [ ]
+ 79
 155
```

27)
```
   78
+ [ ]
 164
```

28)
```
 [ ]
+ 100
 186
```

29)
```
   89
+ [ ]
 175
```

30)
```
 [ ]
+ 91
 162
```

31)
```
   73
+ [ ]
 160
```

32)
```
 [ ]
+ 90
 183
```

33)
```
   78
+ [ ]
 163
```

34)
```
 [ ]
+ 85
 170
```

35)
```
   89
+ [ ]
 160
```

36)
```
 [ ]
+ 81
 159
```

37)
```
   83
+ [ ]
 154
```

38)
```
 [ ]
+ 88
 177
```

39)
```
   90
+ [ ]
 161
```

40)
```
 [ ]
+ 88
 171
```

41)
```
   92
+[ ]
 192
```

42)
```
 [ ]
+ 78
 154
```

43)
```
   96
+ [ ]
 191
```

44)
```
 [ ]
+ 100
 183
```

45)
```
   84
+ [ ]
 178
```

46)
```
 [ ]
+ 80
 156
```

47)
```
   97
+ [ ]
 189
```

48)
```
 [ ]
+ 84
 169
```

49)
```
   93
+ [ ]
 173
```

50)
```
 [ ]
+ 89
 163
```

51)
```
   72
+ [ ]
 153
```

52)
```
 [ ]
+ 89
 169
```

53)
```
   97
+ [ ]
 172
```

54)
```
 [ ]
+ 89
 183
```

55)
```
   75
+ [ ]
 149
```

56)
```
 [ ]
+ 70
 166
```

57)
```
   89
+ [ ]
 174
```

58)
```
 [ ]
+ 93
 176
```

59)
```
   73
+ [ ]
 144
```

60)
```
 [ ]
+ 85
 185
```

1) $73 + \boxed{} = 145$

2) $\boxed{} + 76 = 149$

3) $77 + \boxed{} = 156$

4) $\boxed{} + 99 = 180$

5) $98 + \boxed{} = 192$

6) $\boxed{} + 100 = 179$

7) $86 + \boxed{} = 162$

8) $\boxed{} + 77 = 151$

9) $78 + \boxed{} = 158$

10) $\boxed{} + 86 = 161$

11) $86 + \boxed{} = 181$

12) $\boxed{} + 83 = 156$

13) $74 + \boxed{} = 164$

14) $\boxed{} + 75 = 163$

15) $82 + \boxed{} = 163$

16) $\boxed{} + 91 = 164$

17) $89 + \boxed{} = 185$

18) $\boxed{} + 93 = 168$

19) $75 + \boxed{} = 145$

20) $\boxed{} + 82 = 165$

21) $77 + \boxed{} = 147$

22) $\boxed{} + 79 = 161$

23) $92 + \boxed{} = 192$

24) $\boxed{} + 87 = 159$

25) $92 + \boxed{} = 165$

26) $\boxed{} + 78 = 157$

27) $87 + \boxed{} = 187$

28) $\boxed{} + 70 = 170$

29) $88 + \boxed{} = 166$

30) $\boxed{} + 96 = 186$

31) $93 + \boxed{} = 182$

32) $\boxed{} + 73 = 146$

33) $95 + \boxed{} = 188$

34) $\boxed{} + 80 = 179$

35) $89 + \boxed{} = 171$

36) $\boxed{} + 99 = 191$

37) $90 + \boxed{} = 189$

38) $\boxed{} + 74 = 145$

39) $94 + \boxed{} = 169$

40) $\boxed{} + 76 = 166$

41) $85 + \boxed{} = 183$

42) $\boxed{} + 75 = 146$

43) $100 + \boxed{} = 200$

44) $\boxed{} + 94 = 192$

45) $74 + \boxed{} = 171$

46) $\boxed{} + 88 = 167$

47) $71 + \boxed{} = 156$

48) $\boxed{} + 98 = 180$

49) $99 + \boxed{} = 196$

50) $\boxed{} + 70 = 166$

51) $89 + \boxed{} = 174$

52) $\boxed{} + 94 = 165$

53) $70 + \boxed{} = 164$

54) $\boxed{} + 85 = 184$

55) $79 + \boxed{} = 170$

56) $\boxed{} + 73 = 165$

57) $87 + \boxed{} = 174$

58) $\boxed{} + 86 = 183$

59) $91 + \boxed{} = 177$

60) $\boxed{} + 80 = 155$

1) 84 + ☐ = 162

2) ☐ + 76 = 173

3) 100 + ☐ = 182

4) ☐ + 92 = 182

5) 74 + ☐ = 173

6) ☐ + 83 = 177

7) 71 + ☐ = 165

8) ☐ + 99 = 170

9) 74 + ☐ = 148

10) ☐ + 81 = 155

11) 72 + ☐ = 170

12) ☐ + 78 = 150

13) 91 + ☐ = 184

14) ☐ + 85 = 163

15) 88 + ☐ = 177

16) ☐ + 98 = 188

17) 72 + ☐ = 171

18) ☐ + 100 = 200

19) 79 + ☐ = 155

20) ☐ + 80 = 153

21) 78 + ☐ = 151

22) ☐ + 74 = 165

23) 98 + ☐ = 181

24) ☐ + 95 = 166

25) 77 + ☐ = 154

26) ☐ + 83 = 155

27) 98 + ☐ = 198

28) ☐ + 97 = 171

29) 94 + ☐ = 170

30) ☐ + 89 = 188

31) 92 + ☐ = 174

32) ☐ + 89 = 180

33) 98 + ☐ = 183

34) ☐ + 99 = 183

35) 84 + ☐ = 173

36) ☐ + 91 = 162

37) 82 + ☐ = 168

38) ☐ + 81 = 171

39) 83 + ☐ = 180

40) ☐ + 81 = 177

41) 76 + ☐ = 164

42) ☐ + 92 = 183

43) 94 + ☐ = 164

44) ☐ + 93 = 177

45) 77 + ☐ = 155

46) ☐ + 70 = 145

47) 93 + ☐ = 167

48) ☐ + 93 = 166

49) 94 + ☐ = 182

50) ☐ + 83 = 179

51) 89 + ☐ = 166

52) ☐ + 84 = 182

53) 93 + ☐ = 190

54) ☐ + 91 = 187

55) 71 + ☐ = 166

56) ☐ + 84 = 164

57) 96 + ☐ = 192

58) ☐ + 83 = 175

59) 97 + ☐ = 185

60) ☐ + 74 = 148

1) 77 + ☐ = 165

2) ☐ + 87 = 161

3) 97 + ☐ = 189

4) ☐ + 91 = 183

5) 78 + ☐ = 170

6) ☐ + 97 = 172

7) 88 + ☐ = 159

8) ☐ + 88 = 178

9) 89 + ☐ = 180

10) ☐ + 70 = 166

11) 92 + ☐ = 172

12) ☐ + 78 = 176

13) 87 + ☐ = 164

14) ☐ + 88 = 182

15) 93 + ☐ = 189

16) ☐ + 98 = 190

17) 97 + ☐ = 186

18) ☐ + 77 = 159

19) 74 + ☐ = 158

20) ☐ + 81 = 160

21) 98 + ☐ = 197

22) ☐ + 97 = 191

23) 100 + ☐ = 176

24) ☐ + 85 = 167

25) 90 + ☐ = 185

26) ☐ + 87 = 175

27) 79 + ☐ = 157

28) ☐ + 73 = 152

29) 74 + ☐ = 148

30) ☐ + 93 = 177

31) 85 + ☐ = 181

32) ☐ + 100 = 200

33) 84 + ☐ = 165

34) ☐ + 96 = 168

35) 78 + ☐ = 150

36) ☐ + 77 = 161

37) 74 + ☐ = 167

38) ☐ + 74 = 148

39) 77 + ☐ = 177

40) ☐ + 97 = 167

41) 96 + ☐ = 191

42) ☐ + 100 = 174

43) 92 + ☐ = 169

44) ☐ + 72 = 169

45) 98 + ☐ = 168

46) ☐ + 82 = 160

47) 94 + ☐ = 194

48) ☐ + 70 = 148

49) 81 + ☐ = 152

50) ☐ + 81 = 163

51) 76 + ☐ = 159

52) ☐ + 74 = 165

53) 95 + ☐ = 190

54) ☐ + 73 = 162

55) 93 + ☐ = 175

56) ☐ + 72 = 151

57) 72 + ☐ = 143

58) ☐ + 79 = 167

59) 94 + ☐ = 193

60) ☐ + 95 = 184

1) 86 + ☐ = 178
2) ☐ + 74 = 151
3) 93 + ☐ = 178
4) ☐ + 71 = 149
5) 86 + ☐ = 167
6) ☐ + 71 = 158

7) 75 + ☐ = 151
8) ☐ + 97 = 195
9) 92 + ☐ = 163
10) ☐ + 83 = 182
11) 98 + ☐ = 169
12) ☐ + 100 = 180

13) 87 + ☐ = 165
14) ☐ + 71 = 153
15) 91 + ☐ = 181
16) ☐ + 70 = 152
17) 74 + ☐ = 154
18) ☐ + 74 = 151

19) 95 + ☐ = 180
20) ☐ + 81 = 166
21) 82 + ☐ = 166
22) ☐ + 74 = 166
23) 92 + ☐ = 181
24) ☐ + 86 = 168

25) 79 + ☐ = 150
26) ☐ + 77 = 172
27) 98 + ☐ = 182
28) ☐ + 92 = 180
29) 72 + ☐ = 146
30) ☐ + 91 = 166

31) 89 + ☐ = 183
32) ☐ + 82 = 175
33) 81 + ☐ = 168
34) ☐ + 98 = 198
35) 80 + ☐ = 153
36) ☐ + 76 = 170

37) 84 + ☐ = 181
38) ☐ + 99 = 175
39) 90 + ☐ = 164
40) ☐ + 76 = 148
41) 71 + ☐ = 161
42) ☐ + 70 = 159

43) 74 + ☐ = 148
44) ☐ + 90 = 161
45) 90 + ☐ = 163
46) ☐ + 70 = 158
47) 80 + ☐ = 161
48) ☐ + 97 = 175

49) 93 + ☐ = 169
50) ☐ + 85 = 165
51) 83 + ☐ = 176
52) ☐ + 75 = 167
53) 72 + ☐ = 171
54) ☐ + 74 = 169

55) 76 + ☐ = 154
56) ☐ + 91 = 172
57) 76 + ☐ = 160
58) ☐ + 98 = 172
59) 89 + ☐ = 167
60) ☐ + 77 = 166

1) 105
+ 120

2) 125
+ 110

3) 115
+ 100

4) 113
+ 122

5) 126
+ 110

6) 100
+ 124

7) 117
+ 115

8) 101
+ 117

9) 108
+ 107

10) 112
+ 104

11) 109
+ 110

12) 110
+ 114

13) 108
+ 112

14) 109
+ 116

15) 113
+ 111

16) 110
+ 127

17) 130
+ 121

18) 116
+ 107

19) 129
+ 116

20) 107
+ 126

21) 112
+ 126

22) 125
+ 101

23) 112
+ 102

24) 107
+ 112

25) 111
+ 103

26) 123
+ 122

27) 128
+ 111

28) 127
+ 111

29) 100
+ 109

30) 120
+ 123

31) 113
+ 117

32) 105
+ 115

33) 126
+ 117

34) 128
+ 121

35) 117
+ 126

36) 130
+ 121

37) 123
+ 115

38) 104
+ 100

39) 107
+ 103

40) 119
+ 130

41) 113
+ 102

42) 101
+ 126

43) 119
+ 119

44) 118
+ 130

45) 114
+ 121

46) 122
+ 102

47) 127
+ 119

48) 103
+ 125

49) 109
+ 102

50) 125
+ 107

51) 120
+ 121

52) 115
+ 118

53) 118
+ 100

54) 107
+ 123

55) 127
+ 124

56) 130
+ 130

57) 104
+ 100

58) 119
+ 113

59) 109
+ 114

60) 110
+ 128

Page 32
Time:
Adding Digits 100-130
Name:
Score
/60

1)   106
 + 130

2)   113
 + 109

3)   109
 + 104

4)   110
 + 127

5)   121
 + 104

6)   130
 + 102

7)   122
 + 102

8)   105
 + 108

9)   122
 + 118

10)   101
 + 117

11)   127
 + 130

12)   110
 + 127

13)   119
 + 108

14)   108
 + 129

15)   103
 + 117

16)   121
 + 109

17)   106
 + 107

18)   125
 + 111

19)   121
 + 118

20)   109
 + 115

21)   101
 + 101

22)   123
 + 100

23)   112
 + 117

24)   120
 + 110

25)   103
 + 121

26)   108
 + 115

27)   115
 + 127

28)   126
 + 122

29)   119
 + 115

30)   111
 + 126

31)   106
 + 126

32)   109
 + 108

33)   115
 + 108

34)   114
 + 104

35)   120
 + 104

36)   115
 + 116

37)   129
 + 114

38)   129
 + 105

39)   125
 + 126

40)   123
 + 112

41)   128
 + 124

42)   116
 + 114

43)   109
 + 124

44)   120
 + 126

45)   111
 + 100

46)   115
 + 124

47)   124
 + 125

48)   126
 + 123

49)   116
 + 121

50)   118
 + 130

51)   110
 + 116

52)   113
 + 113

53)   129
 + 107

54)   119
 + 101

55)   109
 + 102

56)   109
 + 128

57)   108
 + 126

58)   102
 + 126

59)   114
 + 128

60)   103
 + 129

1) 130 + 114

2) 113 + 125

3) 112 + 117

4) 112 + 112

5) 122 + 123

6) 105 + 101

7) 129 + 118

8) 118 + 126

9) 118 + 109

10) 113 + 114

11) 122 + 120

12) 121 + 103

13) 106 + 120

14) 104 + 122

15) 106 + 129

16) 126 + 113

17) 101 + 108

18) 117 + 101

19) 129 + 126

20) 102 + 118

21) 123 + 111

22) 113 + 106

23) 101 + 106

24) 128 + 110

25) 108 + 124

26) 101 + 112

27) 129 + 120

28) 124 + 130

29) 105 + 122

30) 129 + 108

31) 125 + 122

32) 102 + 101

33) 129 + 119

34) 128 + 126

35) 120 + 101

36) 126 + 112

37) 123 + 115

38) 103 + 126

39) 113 + 100

40) 111 + 118

41) 102 + 123

42) 101 + 124

43) 105 + 124

44) 100 + 127

45) 116 + 115

46) 105 + 116

47) 130 + 105

48) 102 + 124

49) 113 + 106

50) 126 + 101

51) 117 + 129

52) 124 + 118

53) 100 + 104

54) 113 + 124

55) 109 + 106

56) 129 + 129

57) 122 + 100

58) 129 + 114

59) 106 + 123

60) 104 + 111

1) 106
  + 106

2) 110
  + 102

3) 104
  + 125

4) 114
  + 130

5) 108
  + 115

6) 122
  + 105

7) 108
  + 106

8) 102
  + 114

9) 102
  + 124

10) 115
  + 105

11) 102
  + 105

12) 121
  + 118

13) 128
  + 106

14) 100
  + 110

15) 128
  + 102

16) 103
  + 126

17) 120
  + 128

18) 102
  + 119

19) 102
  + 116

20) 106
  + 115

21) 114
  + 102

22) 114
  + 111

23) 102
  + 110

24) 106
  + 122

25) 123
  + 120

26) 123
  + 107

27) 109
  + 129

28) 123
  + 114

29) 119
  + 121

30) 120
  + 108

31) 123
  + 108

32) 108
  + 120

33) 118
  + 118

34) 127
  + 126

35) 122
  + 112

36) 124
  + 101

37) 121
  + 113

38) 119
  + 109

39) 130
  + 114

40) 110
  + 119

41) 124
  + 127

42) 100
  + 130

43) 122
  + 105

44) 118
  + 105

45) 107
  + 126

46) 130
  + 109

47) 104
  + 101

48) 130
  + 112

49) 114
  + 104

50) 113
  + 129

51) 123
  + 110

52) 121
  + 127

53) 116
  + 106

54) 120
  + 113

55) 122
  + 112

56) 101
  + 123

57) 103
  + 123

58) 104
  + 126

59) 124
  + 111

60) 114
  + 119

1) 107 + 122
2) 100 + 109
3) 114 + 102
4) 116 + 108
5) 110 + 127
6) 108 + 122

7) 122 + 125
8) 126 + 117
9) 100 + 107
10) 128 + 121
11) 106 + 125
12) 100 + 127

13) 120 + 110
14) 124 + 119
15) 125 + 115
16) 130 + 100
17) 121 + 127
18) 103 + 115

19) 117 + 102
20) 100 + 120
21) 119 + 117
22) 116 + 123
23) 110 + 124
24) 101 + 106

25) 125 + 114
26) 121 + 120
27) 109 + 115
28) 128 + 103
29) 116 + 115
30) 119 + 112

31) 109 + 103
32) 128 + 114
33) 108 + 114
34) 127 + 125
35) 127 + 124
36) 118 + 123

37) 119 + 117
38) 105 + 115
39) 122 + 105
40) 101 + 119
41) 114 + 125
42) 111 + 110

43) 112 + 128
44) 105 + 127
45) 127 + 127
46) 119 + 102
47) 111 + 122
48) 102 + 103

49) 100 + 127
50) 105 + 112
51) 126 + 120
52) 121 + 130
53) 113 + 111
54) 109 + 103

55) 117 + 126
56) 126 + 108
57) 116 + 126
58) 121 + 125
59) 100 + 105
60) 100 + 101

1)
```
  112
+ [  ]
─────
  225
```

2)
```
  [  ]
+ 119
─────
  224
```

3)
```
  115
+ [  ]
─────
  221
```

4)
```
  [  ]
+ 107
─────
  212
```

5)
```
  128
+ [  ]
─────
  236
```

6)
```
  [  ]
+ 116
─────
  216
```

7)
```
  119
+ [  ]
─────
  226
```

8)
```
  [  ]
+ 102
─────
  205
```

9)
```
  103
+ [  ]
─────
  204
```

10)
```
  [  ]
+ 107
─────
  213
```

11)
```
  124
+ [  ]
─────
  241
```

12)
```
  [  ]
+ 118
─────
  229
```

13)
```
  119
+ [  ]
─────
  246
```

14)
```
  [  ]
+ 117
─────
  247
```

15)
```
  124
+ [  ]
─────
  243
```

16)
```
  [  ]
+ 107
─────
  221
```

17)
```
  129
+ [  ]
─────
  252
```

18)
```
  [  ]
+ 128
─────
  234
```

19)
```
  114
+ [  ]
─────
  219
```

20)
```
  [  ]
+ 100
─────
  215
```

21)
```
  102
+ [  ]
─────
  232
```

22)
```
  [  ]
+ 115
─────
  229
```

23)
```
  105
+ [  ]
─────
  213
```

24)
```
  [  ]
+ 103
─────
  206
```

25)
```
  105
+ [  ]
─────
  228
```

26)
```
  [  ]
+ 102
─────
  211
```

27)
```
  130
+ [  ]
─────
  245
```

28)
```
  [  ]
+ 115
─────
  241
```

29)
```
  112
+ [  ]
─────
  230
```

30)
```
  [  ]
+ 102
─────
  208
```

31)
```
  119
+ [  ]
─────
  234
```

32)
```
  [  ]
+ 103
─────
  230
```

33)
```
  106
+ [  ]
─────
  216
```

34)
```
  [  ]
+ 125
─────
  237
```

35)
```
  130
+ [  ]
─────
  250
```

36)
```
  [  ]
+ 123
─────
  229
```

37)
```
  125
+ [  ]
─────
  233
```

38)
```
  [  ]
+ 107
─────
  230
```

39)
```
  121
+ [  ]
─────
  236
```

40)
```
  [  ]
+ 101
─────
  227
```

41)
```
  102
+ [  ]
─────
  214
```

42)
```
  [  ]
+ 104
─────
  207
```

43)
```
  124
+ [  ]
─────
  250
```

44)
```
  [  ]
+ 125
─────
  228
```

45)
```
  118
+ [  ]
─────
  239
```

46)
```
  [  ]
+ 123
─────
  234
```

47)
```
  119
+ [  ]
─────
  238
```

48)
```
  [  ]
+ 101
─────
  209
```

49)
```
  102
+ [  ]
─────
  222
```

50)
```
  [  ]
+ 125
─────
  255
```

51)
```
  121
+ [  ]
─────
  232
```

52)
```
  [  ]
+ 108
─────
  217
```

53)
```
  115
+ [  ]
─────
  227
```

54)
```
  [  ]
+ 113
─────
  230
```

55)
```
  128
+ [  ]
─────
  228
```

56)
```
  [  ]
+ 109
─────
  220
```

57)
```
  104
+ [  ]
─────
  211
```

58)
```
  [  ]
+ 129
─────
  241
```

59)
```
  105
+ [  ]
─────
  220
```

60)
```
  [  ]
+ 107
─────
  212
```

1)
$$125 + \boxed{} = 246$$

2)
$$\boxed{} + 103 = 215$$

3)
$$104 + \boxed{} = 211$$

4)
$$\boxed{} + 120 = 227$$

5)
$$102 + \boxed{} = 213$$

6)
$$\boxed{} + 127 = 253$$

7)
$$106 + \boxed{} = 232$$

8)
$$\boxed{} + 117 = 244$$

9)
$$115 + \boxed{} = 215$$

10)
$$\boxed{} + 107 = 210$$

11)
$$120 + \boxed{} = 234$$

12)
$$\boxed{} + 117 = 237$$

13)
$$120 + \boxed{} = 224$$

14)
$$\boxed{} + 112 = 228$$

15)
$$101 + \boxed{} = 223$$

16)
$$\boxed{} + 111 = 219$$

17)
$$113 + \boxed{} = 225$$

18)
$$\boxed{} + 116 = 244$$

19)
$$101 + \boxed{} = 231$$

20)
$$\boxed{} + 115 = 226$$

21)
$$107 + \boxed{} = 214$$

22)
$$\boxed{} + 125 = 228$$

23)
$$116 + \boxed{} = 243$$

24)
$$\boxed{} + 118 = 245$$

25)
$$125 + \boxed{} = 255$$

26)
$$\boxed{} + 117 = 234$$

27)
$$130 + \boxed{} = 235$$

28)
$$\boxed{} + 125 = 253$$

29)
$$129 + \boxed{} = 238$$

30)
$$\boxed{} + 116 = 234$$

31)
$$121 + \boxed{} = 223$$

32)
$$\boxed{} + 103 = 210$$

33)
$$121 + \boxed{} = 239$$

34)
$$\boxed{} + 116 = 227$$

35)
$$101 + \boxed{} = 231$$

36)
$$\boxed{} + 124 = 228$$

37)
$$107 + \boxed{} = 226$$

38)
$$\boxed{} + 128 = 241$$

39)
$$100 + \boxed{} = 205$$

40)
$$\boxed{} + 129 = 238$$

41)
$$129 + \boxed{} = 252$$

42)
$$\boxed{} + 119 = 239$$

43)
$$118 + \boxed{} = 244$$

44)
$$\boxed{} + 107 = 229$$

45)
$$109 + \boxed{} = 218$$

46)
$$\boxed{} + 108 = 228$$

47)
$$116 + \boxed{} = 219$$

48)
$$\boxed{} + 115 = 215$$

49)
$$114 + \boxed{} = 238$$

50)
$$\boxed{} + 105 = 205$$

51)
$$100 + \boxed{} = 214$$

52)
$$\boxed{} + 114 = 234$$

53)
$$116 + \boxed{} = 235$$

54)
$$\boxed{} + 122 = 245$$

55)
$$124 + \boxed{} = 251$$

56)
$$\boxed{} + 118 = 223$$

57)
$$117 + \boxed{} = 220$$

58)
$$\boxed{} + 119 = 220$$

59)
$$123 + \boxed{} = 235$$

60)
$$\boxed{} + 103 = 231$$

1) 102
  + ☐
   217

2) ☐
  + 122
   237

3) 124
  + ☐
   224

4) ☐
  + 121
   221

5) 129
  + ☐
   229

6) ☐
  + 117
   237

7) 111
  + ☐
   239

8) ☐
  + 128
   255

9) 120
  + ☐
   224

10) ☐
   + 112
    227

11) 104
   + ☐
    207

12) ☐
   + 113
    239

13) 124
   + ☐
    249

14) ☐
   + 111
    225

15) 115
   + ☐
    228

16) ☐
   + 101
    230

17) 107
   + ☐
    221

18) ☐
   + 125
    250

19) 101
   + ☐
    217

20) ☐
   + 105
    207

21) 104
   + ☐
    222

22) ☐
   + 106
    236

23) 123
   + ☐
    244

24) ☐
   + 120
    241

25) 108
   + ☐
    234

26) ☐
   + 124
    240

27) 105
   + ☐
    213

28) ☐
   + 102
    229

29) 103
   + ☐
    210

30) ☐
   + 127
    228

31) 101
   + ☐
    225

32) ☐
   + 115
    217

33) 118
   + ☐
    235

34) ☐
   + 126
    228

35) 109
   + ☐
    217

36) ☐
   + 103
    204

37) 103
   + ☐
    219

38) ☐
   + 125
    238

39) 113
   + ☐
    216

40) ☐
   + 109
    238

41) 122
   + ☐
    222

42) ☐
   + 110
    225

43) 121
   + ☐
    243

44) ☐
   + 121
    226

45) 105
   + ☐
    221

46) ☐
   + 105
    226

47) 103
   + ☐
    227

48) ☐
   + 106
    219

49) 112
   + ☐
    213

50) ☐
   + 107
    225

51) 125
   + ☐
    246

52) ☐
   + 117
    232

53) 119
   + ☐
    228

54) ☐
   + 120
    232

55) 109
   + ☐
    215

56) ☐
   + 129
    231

57) 119
   + ☐
    242

58) ☐
   + 108
    230

59) 102
   + ☐
    229

60) ☐
   + 124
    241

1) 100 + ☐ = 216
2) ☐ + 102 = 223
3) 115 + ☐ = 236
4) ☐ + 114 = 225
5) 117 + ☐ = 241
6) ☐ + 110 = 211

7) 111 + ☐ = 225
8) ☐ + 121 = 223
9) 112 + ☐ = 227
10) ☐ + 120 = 247
11) 121 + ☐ = 234
12) ☐ + 113 = 234

13) 114 + ☐ = 236
14) ☐ + 103 = 231
15) 111 + ☐ = 213
16) ☐ + 116 = 221
17) 117 + ☐ = 233
18) ☐ + 117 = 235

19) 127 + ☐ = 246
20) ☐ + 124 = 233
21) 123 + ☐ = 224
22) ☐ + 113 = 234
23) 128 + ☐ = 246
24) ☐ + 113 = 218

25) 115 + ☐ = 223
26) ☐ + 100 = 201
27) 109 + ☐ = 232
28) ☐ + 130 = 243
29) 123 + ☐ = 233
30) ☐ + 122 = 239

31) 130 + ☐ = 250
32) ☐ + 102 = 216
33) 116 + ☐ = 232
34) ☐ + 130 = 230
35) 113 + ☐ = 235
36) ☐ + 106 = 229

37) 111 + ☐ = 239
38) ☐ + 129 = 246
39) 110 + ☐ = 233
40) ☐ + 106 = 229
41) 126 + ☐ = 245
42) ☐ + 100 = 211

43) 125 + ☐ = 235
44) ☐ + 130 = 235
45) 128 + ☐ = 231
46) ☐ + 112 = 220
47) 120 + ☐ = 249
48) ☐ + 116 = 232

49) 117 + ☐ = 247
50) ☐ + 124 = 238
51) 116 + ☐ = 229
52) ☐ + 127 = 232
53) 125 + ☐ = 249
54) ☐ + 111 = 230

55) 121 + ☐ = 228
56) ☐ + 113 = 214
57) 112 + ☐ = 214
58) ☐ + 109 = 237
59) 104 + ☐ = 227
60) ☐ + 100 = 202

1) 118 + ☐ = 228

2) ☐ + 103 = 212

3) 107 + ☐ = 220

4) ☐ + 113 = 213

5) 125 + ☐ = 244

6) ☐ + 111 = 235

7) 122 + ☐ = 252

8) ☐ + 101 = 201

9) 101 + ☐ = 218

10) ☐ + 128 = 233

11) 110 + ☐ = 212

12) ☐ + 103 = 216

13) 101 + ☐ = 224

14) ☐ + 105 = 233

15) 128 + ☐ = 232

16) ☐ + 115 = 230

17) 115 + ☐ = 232

18) ☐ + 100 = 208

19) 114 + ☐ = 240

20) ☐ + 123 = 228

21) 124 + ☐ = 232

22) ☐ + 120 = 239

23) 122 + ☐ = 229

24) ☐ + 112 = 224

25) 113 + ☐ = 217

26) ☐ + 109 = 217

27) 130 + ☐ = 235

28) ☐ + 112 = 228

29) 111 + ☐ = 219

30) ☐ + 110 = 237

31) 112 + ☐ = 229

32) ☐ + 109 = 234

33) 114 + ☐ = 229

34) ☐ + 107 = 209

35) 106 + ☐ = 230

36) ☐ + 118 = 226

37) 104 + ☐ = 229

38) ☐ + 115 = 222

39) 100 + ☐ = 222

40) ☐ + 116 = 229

41) 123 + ☐ = 251

42) ☐ + 101 = 214

43) 130 + ☐ = 237

44) ☐ + 108 = 223

45) 118 + ☐ = 242

46) ☐ + 103 = 227

47) 107 + ☐ = 229

48) ☐ + 100 = 205

49) 126 + ☐ = 238

50) ☐ + 122 = 247

51) 114 + ☐ = 226

52) ☐ + 104 = 217

53) 126 + ☐ = 245

54) ☐ + 116 = 218

55) 105 + ☐ = 207

56) ☐ + 109 = 233

57) 123 + ☐ = 240

58) ☐ + 123 = 230

59) 111 + ☐ = 220

60) ☐ + 118 = 247

1)   157
  + 153

2)   160
  + 134

3)   141
  + 142

4)   155
  + 156

5)   134
  + 139

6)   132
  + 153

7)   139
  + 134

8)   130
  + 134

9)   158
  + 157

10)   144
  + 151

11)   133
  + 160

12)   159
  + 148

13)   152
  + 146

14)   134
  + 143

15)   137
  + 131

16)   137
  + 143

17)   152
  + 142

18)   134
  + 133

19)   152
  + 153

20)   134
  + 142

21)   140
  + 150

22)   148
  + 143

23)   149
  + 154

24)   136
  + 132

25)   156
  + 152

26)   147
  + 151

27)   146
  + 157

28)   131
  + 157

29)   137
  + 155

30)   152
  + 137

31)   143
  + 160

32)   155
  + 142

33)   145
  + 135

34)   132
  + 134

35)   136
  + 155

36)   159
  + 155

37)   141
  + 137

38)   159
  + 156

39)   152
  + 145

40)   149
  + 145

41)   140
  + 142

42)   131
  + 139

43)   160
  + 152

44)   143
  + 151

45)   138
  + 152

46)   144
  + 140

47)   157
  + 158

48)   147
  + 132

49)   159
  + 141

50)   152
  + 151

51)   137
  + 146

52)   145
  + 150

53)   153
  + 151

54)   143
  + 145

55)   158
  + 131

56)   132
  + 133

57)   149
  + 147

58)   134
  + 145

59)   149
  + 131

60)   133
  + 149

1)   148   + 133

2)   134   + 131

3)   147   + 148

4)   150   + 142

5)   130   + 158

6)   154   + 137

7)   153   + 136

8)   144   + 160

9)   132   + 136

10)   130   + 146

11)   154   + 148

12)   151   + 134

13)   148   + 159

14)   151   + 157

15)   155   + 138

16)   147   + 137

17)   149   + 130

18)   144   + 156

19)   144   + 148

20)   147   + 141

21)   132   + 140

22)   139   + 131

23)   133   + 149

24)   148   + 135

25)   147   + 148

26)   158   + 149

27)   156   + 135

28)   153   + 155

29)   158   + 140

30)   131   + 148

31)   160   + 133

32)   148   + 153

33)   145   + 136

34)   151   + 140

35)   159   + 157

36)   136   + 136

37)   137   + 132

38)   141   + 142

39)   141   + 139

40)   147   + 140

41)   130   + 155

42)   158   + 141

43)   152   + 150

44)   132   + 159

45)   158   + 159

46)   141   + 160

47)   131   + 139

48)   130   + 151

49)   142   + 142

50)   154   + 147

51)   137   + 141

52)   136   + 147

53)   148   + 158

54)   141   + 137

55)   135   + 131

56)   149   + 159

57)   144   + 138

58)   140   + 140

59)   148   + 147

60)   150   + 147

1) 138 + 152	2) 136 + 131	3) 151 + 156	4) 131 + 147	5) 156 + 142	6) 135 + 130
7) 145 + 154	8) 138 + 147	9) 147 + 160	10) 157 + 159	11) 140 + 143	12) 160 + 145
13) 145 + 159	14) 146 + 139	15) 153 + 150	16) 133 + 142	17) 134 + 159	18) 147 + 144
19) 131 + 150	20) 152 + 133	21) 131 + 156	22) 152 + 148	23) 134 + 151	24) 146 + 139
25) 131 + 138	26) 148 + 156	27) 135 + 153	28) 158 + 143	29) 155 + 157	30) 145 + 158
31) 141 + 156	32) 157 + 144	33) 130 + 130	34) 149 + 153	35) 140 + 154	36) 139 + 139
37) 158 + 136	38) 155 + 135	39) 156 + 144	40) 143 + 131	41) 149 + 135	42) 131 + 156
43) 143 + 143	44) 137 + 160	45) 159 + 135	46) 149 + 134	47) 144 + 157	48) 154 + 151
49) 152 + 149	50) 150 + 159	51) 132 + 152	52) 150 + 143	53) 155 + 155	54) 144 + 149
55) 152 + 156	56) 144 + 156	57) 155 + 159	58) 158 + 131	59) 146 + 156	60) 151 + 143

1) 149
  + 139

2) 147
  + 154

3) 131
  + 133

4) 148
  + 154

5) 138
  + 153

6) 150
  + 150

7) 144
  + 131

8) 136
  + 138

9) 147
  + 130

10) 138
   + 147

11) 136
   + 143

12) 140
   + 160

13) 152
   + 136

14) 146
   + 149

15) 144
   + 157

16) 158
   + 142

17) 158
   + 160

18) 150
   + 130

19) 145
   + 154

20) 146
   + 130

21) 139
   + 138

22) 149
   + 153

23) 133
   + 152

24) 140
   + 157

25) 135
   + 141

26) 139
   + 152

27) 142
   + 137

28) 155
   + 138

29) 139
   + 159

30) 148
   + 143

31) 156
   + 152

32) 147
   + 155

33) 158
   + 143

34) 143
   + 140

35) 144
   + 138

36) 131
   + 139

37) 149
   + 156

38) 140
   + 150

39) 134
   + 142

40) 135
   + 160

41) 130
   + 147

42) 156
   + 145

43) 143
   + 136

44) 146
   + 130

45) 143
   + 134

46) 148
   + 150

47) 146
   + 144

48) 156
   + 136

49) 137
   + 134

50) 156
   + 155

51) 158
   + 131

52) 134
   + 146

53) 130
   + 144

54) 141
   + 137

55) 147
   + 160

56) 141
   + 137

57) 133
   + 160

58) 152
   + 144

59) 145
   + 138

60) 144
   + 140

1) 145
  + 141

2) 138
  + 145

3) 154
  + 150

4) 139
  + 156

5) 130
  + 156

6) 141
  + 146

7) 131
  + 142

8) 130
  + 158

9) 153
  + 133

10) 140
  + 159

11) 137
  + 144

12) 142
  + 143

13) 130
  + 156

14) 133
  + 130

15) 145
  + 143

16) 134
  + 146

17) 131
  + 149

18) 141
  + 139

19) 154
  + 145

20) 134
  + 135

21) 159
  + 153

22) 139
  + 154

23) 137
  + 148

24) 141
  + 142

25) 136
  + 153

26) 157
  + 157

27) 158
  + 136

28) 142
  + 147

29) 155
  + 141

30) 148
  + 133

31) 160
  + 134

32) 150
  + 148

33) 150
  + 143

34) 158
  + 130

35) 158
  + 135

36) 149
  + 147

37) 130
  + 137

38) 152
  + 131

39) 158
  + 145

40) 147
  + 139

41) 159
  + 147

42) 156
  + 134

43) 141
  + 139

44) 149
  + 155

45) 131
  + 146

46) 159
  + 156

47) 136
  + 156

48) 134
  + 158

49) 150
  + 156

50) 153
  + 131

51) 140
  + 156

52) 145
  + 138

53) 132
  + 147

54) 130
  + 135

55) 135
  + 144

56) 142
  + 131

57) 140
  + 160

58) 131
  + 135

59) 156
  + 160

60) 156
  + 153

1)
```
  142
+ [  ]
-----
  289
```

2)
```
  [  ]
+ 134
-----
  269
```

3)
```
  138
+ [  ]
-----
  280
```

4)
```
  [  ]
+ 159
-----
  317
```

5)
```
  133
+ [  ]
-----
  274
```

6)
```
  [  ]
+ 153
-----
  290
```

7)
```
  145
+ [  ]
-----
  296
```

8)
```
  [  ]
+ 158
-----
  307
```

9)
```
  148
+ [  ]
-----
  305
```

10)
```
  [  ]
+ 140
-----
  280
```

11)
```
  138
+ [  ]
-----
  293
```

12)
```
  [  ]
+ 130
-----
  276
```

13)
```
  144
+ [  ]
-----
  284
```

14)
```
  [  ]
+ 160
-----
  290
```

15)
```
  158
+ [  ]
-----
  307
```

16)
```
  [  ]
+ 155
-----
  299
```

17)
```
  150
+ [  ]
-----
  304
```

18)
```
  [  ]
+ 133
-----
  283
```

19)
```
  146
+ [  ]
-----
  299
```

20)
```
  [  ]
+ 130
-----
  287
```

21)
```
  144
+ [  ]
-----
  303
```

22)
```
  [  ]
+ 150
-----
  299
```

23)
```
  132
+ [  ]
-----
  284
```

24)
```
  [  ]
+ 139
-----
  277
```

25)
```
  136
+ [  ]
-----
  268
```

26)
```
  [  ]
+ 148
-----
  289
```

27)
```
  138
+ [  ]
-----
  294
```

28)
```
  [  ]
+ 134
-----
  275
```

29)
```
  130
+ [  ]
-----
  270
```

30)
```
  [  ]
+ 134
-----
  275
```

31)
```
  151
+ [  ]
-----
  282
```

32)
```
  [  ]
+ 147
-----
  277
```

33)
```
  159
+ [  ]
-----
  303
```

34)
```
  [  ]
+ 131
-----
  291
```

35)
```
  150
+ [  ]
-----
  299
```

36)
```
  [  ]
+ 136
-----
  286
```

37)
```
  153
+ [  ]
-----
  288
```

38)
```
  [  ]
+ 140
-----
  287
```

39)
```
  153
+ [  ]
-----
  287
```

40)
```
  [  ]
+ 159
-----
  294
```

41)
```
  154
+ [  ]
-----
  300
```

42)
```
  [  ]
+ 156
-----
  297
```

43)
```
  151
+ [  ]
-----
  311
```

44)
```
  [  ]
+ 157
-----
  291
```

45)
```
  155
+ [  ]
-----
  289
```

46)
```
  [  ]
+ 154
-----
  293
```

47)
```
  154
+ [  ]
-----
  305
```

48)
```
  [  ]
+ 133
-----
  279
```

49)
```
  151
+ [  ]
-----
  311
```

50)
```
  [  ]
+ 140
-----
  276
```

51)
```
  149
+ [  ]
-----
  295
```

52)
```
  [  ]
+ 153
-----
  296
```

53)
```
  158
+ [  ]
-----
  316
```

54)
```
  [  ]
+ 156
-----
  305
```

55)
```
  130
+ [  ]
-----
  272
```

56)
```
  [  ]
+ 132
-----
  276
```

57)
```
  138
+ [  ]
-----
  278
```

58)
```
  [  ]
+ 147
-----
  297
```

59)
```
  135
+ [  ]
-----
  267
```

60)
```
  [  ]
+ 147
-----
  306
```

1) 144
  + ☐
    303

2) ☐
  + 132
    278

3) 142
  + ☐
    291

4) ☐
  + 139
    291

5) 146
  + ☐
    299

6) ☐
  + 160
    315

7) 142
  + ☐
    280

8) ☐
  + 150
    280

9) 149
  + ☐
    281

10) ☐
  + 158
    318

11) 151
  + ☐
    288

12) ☐
  + 160
    291

13) 156
  + ☐
    286

14) ☐
  + 149
    304

15) 130
  + ☐
    274

16) ☐
  + 136
    278

17) 145
  + ☐
    297

18) ☐
  + 148
    300

19) 151
  + ☐
    289

20) ☐
  + 133
    266

21) 158
  + ☐
    308

22) ☐
  + 133
    282

23) 152
  + ☐
    292

24) ☐
  + 159
    303

25) 132
  + ☐
    267

26) ☐
  + 143
    296

27) 157
  + ☐
    297

28) ☐
  + 141
    272

29) 160
  + ☐
    303

30) ☐
  + 139
    293

31) 156
  + ☐
    292

32) ☐
  + 146
    278

33) 135
  + ☐
    278

34) ☐
  + 148
    280

35) 149
  + ☐
    294

36) ☐
  + 142
    277

37) 143
  + ☐
    276

38) ☐
  + 150
    295

39) 152
  + ☐
    299

40) ☐
  + 140
    295

41) 160
  + ☐
    296

42) ☐
  + 148
    290

43) 139
  + ☐
    287

44) ☐
  + 133
    273

45) 144
  + ☐
    296

46) ☐
  + 144
    302

47) 150
  + ☐
    297

48) ☐
  + 134
    280

49) 153
  + ☐
    307

50) ☐
  + 139
    293

51) 131
  + ☐
    288

52) ☐
  + 157
    301

53) 156
  + ☐
    305

54) ☐
  + 158
    304

55) 154
  + ☐
    290

56) ☐
  + 147
    279

57) 148
  + ☐
    304

58) ☐
  + 159
    312

59) 145
  + ☐
    300

60) ☐
  + 146
    289

1) 151 + ___ = 297

2) ___ + 138 = 279

3) 158 + ___ = 308

4) ___ + 132 = 276

5) 146 + ___ = 287

6) ___ + 156 = 316

7) 132 + ___ = 274

8) ___ + 157 = 301

9) 158 + ___ = 301

10) ___ + 147 = 291

11) 131 + ___ = 284

12) ___ + 157 = 299

13) 145 + ___ = 294

14) ___ + 142 = 287

15) 151 + ___ = 284

16) ___ + 130 = 273

17) 139 + ___ = 299

18) ___ + 160 = 305

19) 135 + ___ = 286

20) ___ + 152 = 309

21) 136 + ___ = 288

22) ___ + 159 = 302

23) 154 + ___ = 302

24) ___ + 145 = 295

25) 157 + ___ = 308

26) ___ + 150 = 308

27) 151 + ___ = 290

28) ___ + 152 = 306

29) 149 + ___ = 281

30) ___ + 146 = 295

31) 134 + ___ = 275

32) ___ + 150 = 303

33) 135 + ___ = 266

34) ___ + 130 = 273

35) 157 + ___ = 316

36) ___ + 138 = 275

37) 141 + ___ = 291

38) ___ + 135 = 281

39) 131 + ___ = 290

40) ___ + 160 = 300

41) 138 + ___ = 274

42) ___ + 157 = 306

43) 145 + ___ = 281

44) ___ + 146 = 284

45) 159 + ___ = 311

46) ___ + 151 = 293

47) 147 + ___ = 303

48) ___ + 135 = 287

49) 134 + ___ = 294

50) ___ + 138 = 290

51) 149 + ___ = 284

52) ___ + 146 = 298

53) 142 + ___ = 300

54) ___ + 147 = 303

55) 142 + ___ = 295

56) ___ + 160 = 298

57) 150 + ___ = 305

58) ___ + 157 = 292

59) 155 + ___ = 307

60) ___ + 154 = 289

1)
```
  146
+ [  ]
-----
  283
```

2)
```
  [  ]
+ 136
-----
  288
```

3)
```
  137
+ [  ]
-----
  284
```

4)
```
  [  ]
+ 150
-----
  306
```

5)
```
  147
+ [  ]
-----
  281
```

6)
```
  [  ]
+ 149
-----
  283
```

7)
```
  156
+ [  ]
-----
  297
```

8)
```
  [  ]
+ 131
-----
  271
```

9)
```
  148
+ [  ]
-----
  289
```

10)
```
  [  ]
+ 152
-----
  296
```

11)
```
  135
+ [  ]
-----
  287
```

12)
```
  [  ]
+ 130
-----
  268
```

13)
```
  150
+ [  ]
-----
  295
```

14)
```
  [  ]
+ 141
-----
  281
```

15)
```
  142
+ [  ]
-----
  290
```

16)
```
  [  ]
+ 140
-----
  277
```

17)
```
  137
+ [  ]
-----
  280
```

18)
```
  [  ]
+ 140
-----
  278
```

19)
```
  131
+ [  ]
-----
  278
```

20)
```
  [  ]
+ 144
-----
  297
```

21)
```
  152
+ [  ]
-----
  293
```

22)
```
  [  ]
+ 139
-----
  278
```

23)
```
  157
+ [  ]
-----
  310
```

24)
```
  [  ]
+ 141
-----
  278
```

25)
```
  143
+ [  ]
-----
  273
```

26)
```
  [  ]
+ 144
-----
  296
```

27)
```
  156
+ [  ]
-----
  292
```

28)
```
  [  ]
+ 134
-----
  283
```

29)
```
  146
+ [  ]
-----
  290
```

30)
```
  [  ]
+ 140
-----
  289
```

31)
```
  148
+ [  ]
-----
  297
```

32)
```
  [  ]
+ 155
-----
  300
```

33)
```
  154
+ [  ]
-----
  306
```

34)
```
  [  ]
+ 144
-----
  289
```

35)
```
  136
+ [  ]
-----
  270
```

36)
```
  [  ]
+ 137
-----
  286
```

37)
```
  134
+ [  ]
-----
  277
```

38)
```
  [  ]
+ 137
-----
  268
```

39)
```
  159
+ [  ]
-----
  319
```

40)
```
  [  ]
+ 140
-----
  297
```

41)
```
  147
+ [  ]
-----
  306
```

42)
```
  [  ]
+ 136
-----
  270
```

43)
```
  130
+ [  ]
-----
  285
```

44)
```
  [  ]
+ 133
-----
  274
```

45)
```
  148
+ [  ]
-----
  286
```

46)
```
  [  ]
+ 131
-----
  261
```

47)
```
  132
+ [  ]
-----
  282
```

48)
```
  [  ]
+ 146
-----
  298
```

49)
```
  144
+ [  ]
-----
  281
```

50)
```
  [  ]
+ 131
-----
  281
```

51)
```
  139
+ [  ]
-----
  288
```

52)
```
  [  ]
+ 143
-----
  294
```

53)
```
  145
+ [  ]
-----
  301
```

54)
```
  [  ]
+ 138
-----
  295
```

55)
```
  144
+ [  ]
-----
  298
```

56)
```
  [  ]
+ 143
-----
  302
```

57)
```
  154
+ [  ]
-----
  297
```

58)
```
  [  ]
+ 156
-----
  289
```

59)
```
  131
+ [  ]
-----
  263
```

60)
```
  [  ]
+ 151
-----
  293
```

1) 140
  + [ ]
  = 281

2) [ ]
  + 131
  = 270

3) 143
  + [ ]
  = 295

4) [ ]
  + 157
  = 290

5) 141
  + [ ]
  = 275

6) [ ]
  + 134
  = 282

7) 131
  + [ ]
  = 276

8) [ ]
  + 141
  = 288

9) 155
  + [ ]
  = 308

10) [ ]
  + 150
  = 301

11) 147
  + [ ]
  = 278

12) [ ]
  + 158
  = 312

13) 141
  + [ ]
  = 276

14) [ ]
  + 149
  = 279

15) 149
  + [ ]
  = 281

16) [ ]
  + 154
  = 292

17) 156
  + [ ]
  = 301

18) [ ]
  + 149
  = 288

19) 140
  + [ ]
  = 294

20) [ ]
  + 154
  = 298

21) 147
  + [ ]
  = 297

22) [ ]
  + 137
  = 285

23) 133
  + [ ]
  = 269

24) [ ]
  + 143
  = 297

25) 149
  + [ ]
  = 287

26) [ ]
  + 160
  = 303

27) 148
  + [ ]
  = 292

28) [ ]
  + 140
  = 299

29) 153
  + [ ]
  = 284

30) [ ]
  + 156
  = 286

31) 141
  + [ ]
  = 300

32) [ ]
  + 133
  = 282

33) 153
  + [ ]
  = 312

34) [ ]
  + 150
  = 280

35) 137
  + [ ]
  = 277

36) [ ]
  + 153
  = 304

37) 148
  + [ ]
  = 282

38) [ ]
  + 132
  = 275

39) 132
  + [ ]
  = 288

40) [ ]
  + 155
  = 315

41) 154
  + [ ]
  = 296

42) [ ]
  + 145
  = 284

43) 145
  + [ ]
  = 283

44) [ ]
  + 140
  = 287

45) 148
  + [ ]
  = 298

46) [ ]
  + 154
  = 288

47) 133
  + [ ]
  = 284

48) [ ]
  + 134
  = 294

49) 132
  + [ ]
  = 282

50) [ ]
  + 130
  = 279

51) 154
  + [ ]
  = 296

52) [ ]
  + 131
  = 261

53) 145
  + [ ]
  = 304

54) [ ]
  + 133
  = 284

55) 135
  + [ ]
  = 275

56) [ ]
  + 131
  = 282

57) 151
  + [ ]
  = 288

58) [ ]
  + 160
  = 314

59) 154
  + [ ]
  = 307

60) [ ]
  + 152
  = 297

1) 36
  − 35

2) 38
  − 38

3) 35
  − 10

4) 37
  − 33

5) 38
  − 30

6) 28
  − 28

7) 18
  − 13

8) 30
  − 22

9) 16
  − 14

10) 33
  − 14

11) 30
  − 25

12) 24
  − 24

13) 39
  − 31

14) 23
  − 14

15) 29
  − 15

16) 37
  − 18

17) 36
  − 35

18) 35
  − 15

19) 34
  − 14

20) 12
  − 12

21) 26
  − 11

22) 37
  − 14

23) 38
  − 37

24) 23
  − 12

25) 29
  − 22

26) 19
  − 15

27) 18
  − 12

28) 27
  − 20

29) 37
  − 11

30) 40
  − 34

31) 32
  − 19

32) 30
  − 10

33) 37
  − 21

34) 30
  − 17

35) 37
  − 11

36) 23
  − 14

37) 32
  − 12

38) 38
  − 21

39) 27
  − 17

40) 21
  − 13

41) 33
  − 18

42) 28
  − 25

43) 29
  − 19

44) 24
  − 14

45) 21
  − 18

46) 33
  − 12

47) 37
  − 35

48) 40
  − 35

49) 33
  − 13

50) 36
  − 32

51) 29
  − 19

52) 34
  − 15

53) 40
  − 21

54) 30
  − 11

55) 34
  − 18

56) 30
  − 19

57) 16
  − 14

58) 19
  − 10

59) 20
  − 16

60) 13
  − 10

1) 22 − 20

2) 38 − 35

3) 32 − 24

4) 35 − 15

5) 38 − 28

6) 40 − 38

7) 24 − 19

8) 16 − 16

9) 38 − 26

10) 23 − 13

11) 19 − 17

12) 31 − 16

13) 40 − 31

14) 18 − 14

15) 35 − 33

16) 21 − 10

17) 32 − 30

18) 38 − 24

19) 39 − 31

20) 35 − 30

21) 27 − 12

22) 31 − 25

23) 36 − 28

24) 39 − 34

25) 33 − 26

26) 14 − 13

27) 25 − 21

28) 34 − 31

29) 21 − 19

30) 26 − 10

31) 34 − 12

32) 40 − 23

33) 34 − 22

34) 29 − 17

35) 31 − 10

36) 39 − 36

37) 13 − 10

38) 31 − 16

39) 30 − 22

40) 23 − 18

41) 17 − 14

42) 39 − 28

43) 37 − 30

44) 37 − 20

45) 35 − 25

46) 32 − 24

47) 22 − 21

48) 31 − 20

49) 39 − 19

50) 32 − 29

51) 16 − 12

52) 24 − 20

53) 31 − 16

54) 19 − 17

55) 36 − 22

56) 22 − 19

57) 28 − 14

58) 37 − 14

59) 32 − 14

60) 39 − 18

1) $25 - 18$ 2) $23 - 13$ 3) $37 - 11$ 4) $35 - 32$ 5) $28 - 28$ 6) $27 - 26$

7) $21 - 12$ 8) $30 - 25$ 9) $11 - 10$ 10) $40 - 32$ 11) $34 - 19$ 12) $35 - 10$

13) $39 - 39$ 14) $39 - 18$ 15) $24 - 11$ 16) $33 - 19$ 17) $29 - 18$ 18) $38 - 25$

19) $19 - 15$ 20) $24 - 14$ 21) $26 - 16$ 22) $19 - 15$ 23) $23 - 18$ 24) $28 - 21$

25) $33 - 28$ 26) $23 - 20$ 27) $34 - 27$ 28) $38 - 10$ 29) $35 - 17$ 30) $24 - 10$

31) $25 - 13$ 32) $23 - 14$ 33) $25 - 19$ 34) $32 - 24$ 35) $16 - 11$ 36) $18 - 14$

37) $40 - 10$ 38) $19 - 14$ 39) $26 - 21$ 40) $37 - 27$ 41) $33 - 27$ 42) $38 - 20$

43) $36 - 11$ 44) $29 - 15$ 45) $34 - 19$ 46) $39 - 10$ 47) $37 - 24$ 48) $40 - 23$

49) $39 - 18$ 50) $39 - 12$ 51) $13 - 12$ 52) $39 - 29$ 53) $38 - 25$ 54) $40 - 27$

55) $34 - 33$ 56) $30 - 26$ 57) $39 - 24$ 58) $16 - 11$ 59) $31 - 11$ 60) $17 - 13$

1) 37 − 23

2) 30 − 24

3) 36 − 17

4) 39 − 19

5) 35 − 27

6) 31 − 26

7) 27 − 27

8) 22 − 10

9) 37 − 12

10) 13 − 12

11) 40 − 37

12) 29 − 11

13) 32 − 31

14) 35 − 11

15) 38 − 35

16) 40 − 19

17) 34 − 28

18) 14 − 13

19) 20 − 15

20) 17 − 14

21) 32 − 25

22) 23 − 10

23) 30 − 17

24) 26 − 21

25) 22 − 16

26) 13 − 13

27) 35 − 18

28) 31 − 18

29) 16 − 13

30) 13 − 10

31) 22 − 19

32) 33 − 29

33) 39 − 14

34) 26 − 11

35) 40 − 20

36) 32 − 11

37) 36 − 33

38) 26 − 22

39) 18 − 16

40) 34 − 17

41) 26 − 26

42) 34 − 30

43) 38 − 15

44) 34 − 25

45) 29 − 16

46) 17 − 11

47) 37 − 33

48) 18 − 14

49) 37 − 29

50) 19 − 16

51) 33 − 18

52) 19 − 14

53) 26 − 12

54) 25 − 13

55) 39 − 33

56) 21 − 11

57) 39 − 38

58) 39 − 26

59) 24 − 20

60) 29 − 28

1) 23 − 19
2) 38 − 37
3) 40 − 38
4) 40 − 30
5) 33 − 31
6) 29 − 12

7) 34 − 28
8) 36 − 22
9) 40 − 33
10) 38 − 16
11) 27 − 27
12) 27 − 17

13) 38 − 21
14) 36 − 12
15) 40 − 27
16) 19 − 16
17) 28 − 16
18) 14 − 14

19) 29 − 24
20) 14 − 13
21) 34 − 26
22) 33 − 19
23) 31 − 25
24) 29 − 25

25) 37 − 28
26) 34 − 26
27) 23 − 14
28) 32 − 19
29) 28 − 11
30) 34 − 13

31) 38 − 29
32) 27 − 19
33) 37 − 29
34) 32 − 29
35) 40 − 17
36) 33 − 30

37) 38 − 12
38) 19 − 15
39) 33 − 21
40) 18 − 12
41) 36 − 15
42) 17 − 10

43) 38 − 19
44) 37 − 14
45) 24 − 12
46) 37 − 17
47) 31 − 17
48) 39 − 35

49) 37 − 26
50) 38 − 25
51) 18 − 14
52) 23 − 12
53) 25 − 22
54) 23 − 16

55) 34 − 19
56) 26 − 25
57) 16 − 12
58) 24 − 23
59) 24 − 16
60) 27 − 25

1) 29
  − ☐
  10

2) ☐
  − 18
  0

3) 39
  − ☐
  27

4) ☐
  − 10
  15

5) 31
  − ☐
  21

6) ☐
  − 24
  11

7) 18
  − ☐
  2

8) ☐
  − 26
  3

9) 21
  − ☐
  1

10) ☐
  − 12
  24

11) 35
  − ☐
  4

12) ☐
  − 18
  17

13) 39
  − ☐
  5

14) ☐
  − 27
  10

15) 29
  − ☐
  4

16) ☐
  − 18
  1

17) 32
  − ☐
  18

18) ☐
  − 10
  7

19) 35
  − ☐
  2

20) ☐
  − 15
  9

21) 36
  − ☐
  8

22) ☐
  − 15
  0

23) 26
  − ☐
  8

24) ☐
  − 18
  10

25) 24
  − ☐
  6

26) ☐
  − 20
  15

27) 24
  − ☐
  13

28) ☐
  − 10
  21

29) 32
  − ☐
  22

30) ☐
  − 16
  15

31) 18
  − ☐
  8

32) ☐
  − 33
  3

33) 26
  − ☐
  7

34) ☐
  − 11
  24

35) 39
  − ☐
  28

36) ☐
  − 29
  4

37) 33
  − ☐
  23

38) ☐
  − 25
  7

39) 28
  − ☐
  15

40) ☐
  − 23
  8

41) 15
  − ☐
  2

42) ☐
  − 13
  18

43) 38
  − ☐
  13

44) ☐
  − 15
  17

45) 34
  − ☐
  13

46) ☐
  − 28
  7

47) 35
  − ☐
  10

48) ☐
  − 18
  22

49) 28
  − ☐
  3

50) ☐
  − 16
  3

51) 31
  − ☐
  10

52) ☐
  − 24
  3

53) 30
  − ☐
  12

54) ☐
  − 17
  18

55) 35
  − ☐
  22

56) ☐
  − 31
  3

57) 39
  − ☐
  23

58) ☐
  − 34
  3

59) 30
  − ☐
  19

60) ☐
  − 10
  28

1) 31 − ☐ = 20

2) ☐ − 26 = 13

3) 31 − ☐ = 2

4) ☐ − 14 = 18

5) 26 − ☐ = 5

6) ☐ − 23 = 9

7) 23 − ☐ = 4

8) ☐ − 30 = 9

9) 32 − ☐ = 17

10) ☐ − 29 = 3

11) 40 − ☐ = 18

12) ☐ − 30 = 7

13) 39 − ☐ = 20

14) ☐ − 15 = 22

15) 32 − ☐ = 3

16) ☐ − 12 = 15

17) 22 − ☐ = 11

18) ☐ − 29 = 0

19) 38 − ☐ = 2

20) ☐ − 35 = 1

21) 31 − ☐ = 8

22) ☐ − 10 = 3

23) 26 − ☐ = 13

24) ☐ − 35 = 4

25) 27 − ☐ = 6

26) ☐ − 25 = 7

27) 20 − ☐ = 4

28) ☐ − 33 = 0

29) 31 − ☐ = 19

30) ☐ − 27 = 2

31) 39 − ☐ = 11

32) ☐ − 34 = 1

33) 36 − ☐ = 10

34) ☐ − 10 = 0

35) 37 − ☐ = 7

36) ☐ − 15 = 15

37) 28 − ☐ = 14

38) ☐ − 11 = 29

39) 34 − ☐ = 15

40) ☐ − 15 = 2

41) 27 − ☐ = 5

42) ☐ − 29 = 7

43) 34 − ☐ = 4

44) ☐ − 29 = 7

45) 33 − ☐ = 20

46) ☐ − 14 = 13

47) 26 − ☐ = 8

48) ☐ − 15 = 2

49) 33 − ☐ = 17

50) ☐ − 34 = 4

51) 34 − ☐ = 12

52) ☐ − 33 = 0

53) 39 − ☐ = 2

54) ☐ − 21 = 14

55) 38 − ☐ = 1

56) ☐ − 32 = 8

57) 33 − ☐ = 12

58) ☐ − 17 = 12

59) 26 − ☐ = 14

60) ☐ − 21 = 0

1) 33 − ☐ = 17

2) ☐ − 31 = 5

3) 38 − ☐ = 28

4) ☐ − 29 = 7

5) 28 − ☐ = 4

6) ☐ − 24 = 15

7) 29 − ☐ = 1

8) ☐ − 14 = 2

9) 24 − ☐ = 11

10) ☐ − 18 = 9

11) 39 − ☐ = 11

12) ☐ − 16 = 18

13) 40 − ☐ = 11

14) ☐ − 20 = 10

15) 31 − ☐ = 19

16) ☐ − 21 = 8

17) 31 − ☐ = 19

18) ☐ − 26 = 8

19) 26 − ☐ = 15

20) ☐ − 20 = 9

21) 36 − ☐ = 10

22) ☐ − 27 = 1

23) 32 − ☐ = 3

24) ☐ − 13 = 1

25) 33 − ☐ = 12

26) ☐ − 21 = 2

27) 33 − ☐ = 19

28) ☐ − 16 = 6

29) 40 − ☐ = 2

30) ☐ − 31 = 3

31) 37 − ☐ = 26

32) ☐ − 23 = 9

33) 37 − ☐ = 15

34) ☐ − 17 = 9

35) 38 − ☐ = 26

36) ☐ − 10 = 14

37) 39 − ☐ = 8

38) ☐ − 30 = 8

39) 38 − ☐ = 7

40) ☐ − 12 = 28

41) 31 − ☐ = 7

42) ☐ − 32 = 4

43) 23 − ☐ = 6

44) ☐ − 19 = 4

45) 30 − ☐ = 1

46) ☐ − 17 = 4

47) 28 − ☐ = 8

48) ☐ − 17 = 18

49) 22 − ☐ = 8

50) ☐ − 18 = 13

51) 36 − ☐ = 10

52) ☐ − 13 = 2

53) 33 − ☐ = 18

54) ☐ − 11 = 0

55) 16 − ☐ = 6

56) ☐ − 33 = 5

57) 36 − ☐ = 1

58) ☐ − 12 = 16

59) 25 − ☐ = 5

60) ☐ − 29 = 10

1)
$$\begin{array}{r} 38 \\ - \boxed{} \\ \hline 15 \end{array}$$

2)
$$\begin{array}{r} \boxed{} \\ - 17 \\ \hline 19 \end{array}$$

3)
$$\begin{array}{r} 34 \\ - \boxed{} \\ \hline 6 \end{array}$$

4)
$$\begin{array}{r} \boxed{} \\ - 17 \\ \hline 16 \end{array}$$

5)
$$\begin{array}{r} 28 \\ - \boxed{} \\ \hline 14 \end{array}$$

6)
$$\begin{array}{r} \boxed{} \\ - 15 \\ \hline 17 \end{array}$$

7)
$$\begin{array}{r} 22 \\ - \boxed{} \\ \hline 8 \end{array}$$

8)
$$\begin{array}{r} \boxed{} \\ - 34 \\ \hline 0 \end{array}$$

9)
$$\begin{array}{r} 36 \\ - \boxed{} \\ \hline 5 \end{array}$$

10)
$$\begin{array}{r} \boxed{} \\ - 21 \\ \hline 13 \end{array}$$

11)
$$\begin{array}{r} 29 \\ - \boxed{} \\ \hline 7 \end{array}$$

12)
$$\begin{array}{r} \boxed{} \\ - 16 \\ \hline 24 \end{array}$$

13)
$$\begin{array}{r} 18 \\ - \boxed{} \\ \hline 0 \end{array}$$

14)
$$\begin{array}{r} \boxed{} \\ - 12 \\ \hline 24 \end{array}$$

15)
$$\begin{array}{r} 27 \\ - \boxed{} \\ \hline 1 \end{array}$$

16)
$$\begin{array}{r} \boxed{} \\ - 21 \\ \hline 7 \end{array}$$

17)
$$\begin{array}{r} 14 \\ - \boxed{} \\ \hline 2 \end{array}$$

18)
$$\begin{array}{r} \boxed{} \\ - 30 \\ \hline 8 \end{array}$$

19)
$$\begin{array}{r} 34 \\ - \boxed{} \\ \hline 22 \end{array}$$

20)
$$\begin{array}{r} \boxed{} \\ - 29 \\ \hline 5 \end{array}$$

21)
$$\begin{array}{r} 10 \\ - \boxed{} \\ \hline 0 \end{array}$$

22)
$$\begin{array}{r} \boxed{} \\ - 23 \\ \hline 11 \end{array}$$

23)
$$\begin{array}{r} 18 \\ - \boxed{} \\ \hline 7 \end{array}$$

24)
$$\begin{array}{r} \boxed{} \\ - 37 \\ \hline 1 \end{array}$$

25)
$$\begin{array}{r} 25 \\ - \boxed{} \\ \hline 10 \end{array}$$

26)
$$\begin{array}{r} \boxed{} \\ - 16 \\ \hline 23 \end{array}$$

27)
$$\begin{array}{r} 33 \\ - \boxed{} \\ \hline 9 \end{array}$$

28)
$$\begin{array}{r} \boxed{} \\ - 14 \\ \hline 1 \end{array}$$

29)
$$\begin{array}{r} 28 \\ - \boxed{} \\ \hline 0 \end{array}$$

30)
$$\begin{array}{r} \boxed{} \\ - 34 \\ \hline 6 \end{array}$$

31)
$$\begin{array}{r} 38 \\ - \boxed{} \\ \hline 20 \end{array}$$

32)
$$\begin{array}{r} \boxed{} \\ - 17 \\ \hline 14 \end{array}$$

33)
$$\begin{array}{r} 36 \\ - \boxed{} \\ \hline 17 \end{array}$$

34)
$$\begin{array}{r} \boxed{} \\ - 18 \\ \hline 13 \end{array}$$

35)
$$\begin{array}{r} 18 \\ - \boxed{} \\ \hline 6 \end{array}$$

36)
$$\begin{array}{r} \boxed{} \\ - 14 \\ \hline 23 \end{array}$$

37)
$$\begin{array}{r} 33 \\ - \boxed{} \\ \hline 10 \end{array}$$

38)
$$\begin{array}{r} \boxed{} \\ - 22 \\ \hline 14 \end{array}$$

39)
$$\begin{array}{r} 36 \\ - \boxed{} \\ \hline 4 \end{array}$$

40)
$$\begin{array}{r} \boxed{} \\ - 12 \\ \hline 10 \end{array}$$

41)
$$\begin{array}{r} 34 \\ - \boxed{} \\ \hline 7 \end{array}$$

42)
$$\begin{array}{r} \boxed{} \\ - 25 \\ \hline 4 \end{array}$$

43)
$$\begin{array}{r} 20 \\ - \boxed{} \\ \hline 6 \end{array}$$

44)
$$\begin{array}{r} \boxed{} \\ - 36 \\ \hline 4 \end{array}$$

45)
$$\begin{array}{r} 15 \\ - \boxed{} \\ \hline 5 \end{array}$$

46)
$$\begin{array}{r} \boxed{} \\ - 31 \\ \hline 6 \end{array}$$

47)
$$\begin{array}{r} 30 \\ - \boxed{} \\ \hline 15 \end{array}$$

48)
$$\begin{array}{r} \boxed{} \\ - 16 \\ \hline 7 \end{array}$$

49)
$$\begin{array}{r} 13 \\ - \boxed{} \\ \hline 1 \end{array}$$

50)
$$\begin{array}{r} \boxed{} \\ - 17 \\ \hline 10 \end{array}$$

51)
$$\begin{array}{r} 22 \\ - \boxed{} \\ \hline 6 \end{array}$$

52)
$$\begin{array}{r} \boxed{} \\ - 28 \\ \hline 0 \end{array}$$

53)
$$\begin{array}{r} 37 \\ - \boxed{} \\ \hline 7 \end{array}$$

54)
$$\begin{array}{r} \boxed{} \\ - 22 \\ \hline 14 \end{array}$$

55)
$$\begin{array}{r} 33 \\ - \boxed{} \\ \hline 20 \end{array}$$

56)
$$\begin{array}{r} \boxed{} \\ - 32 \\ \hline 1 \end{array}$$

57)
$$\begin{array}{r} 30 \\ - \boxed{} \\ \hline 12 \end{array}$$

58)
$$\begin{array}{r} \boxed{} \\ - 10 \\ \hline 29 \end{array}$$

59)
$$\begin{array}{r} 31 \\ - \boxed{} \\ \hline 8 \end{array}$$

60)
$$\begin{array}{r} \boxed{} \\ - 13 \\ \hline 24 \end{array}$$

1) $\begin{array}{r} 32 \\ -\ \boxed{} \\ \hline 20 \end{array}$	2) $\begin{array}{r} \boxed{} \\ -\ 13 \\ \hline 27 \end{array}$	3) $\begin{array}{r} 17 \\ -\ \boxed{} \\ \hline 5 \end{array}$	4) $\begin{array}{r} \boxed{} \\ -\ 13 \\ \hline 14 \end{array}$	5) $\begin{array}{r} 19 \\ -\ \boxed{} \\ \hline 3 \end{array}$	6) $\begin{array}{r} \boxed{} \\ -\ 31 \\ \hline 9 \end{array}$
7) $\begin{array}{r} 40 \\ -\ \boxed{} \\ \hline 1 \end{array}$	8) $\begin{array}{r} \boxed{} \\ -\ 27 \\ \hline 10 \end{array}$	9) $\begin{array}{r} 28 \\ -\ \boxed{} \\ \hline 8 \end{array}$	10) $\begin{array}{r} \boxed{} \\ -\ 14 \\ \hline 16 \end{array}$	11) $\begin{array}{r} 30 \\ -\ \boxed{} \\ \hline 4 \end{array}$	12) $\begin{array}{r} \boxed{} \\ -\ 26 \\ \hline 0 \end{array}$
13) $\begin{array}{r} 35 \\ -\ \boxed{} \\ \hline 23 \end{array}$	14) $\begin{array}{r} \boxed{} \\ -\ 19 \\ \hline 0 \end{array}$	15) $\begin{array}{r} 15 \\ -\ \boxed{} \\ \hline 5 \end{array}$	16) $\begin{array}{r} \boxed{} \\ -\ 10 \\ \hline 1 \end{array}$	17) $\begin{array}{r} 22 \\ -\ \boxed{} \\ \hline 1 \end{array}$	18) $\begin{array}{r} \boxed{} \\ -\ 10 \\ \hline 26 \end{array}$
19) $\begin{array}{r} 20 \\ -\ \boxed{} \\ \hline 9 \end{array}$	20) $\begin{array}{r} \boxed{} \\ -\ 27 \\ \hline 11 \end{array}$	21) $\begin{array}{r} 37 \\ -\ \boxed{} \\ \hline 5 \end{array}$	22) $\begin{array}{r} \boxed{} \\ -\ 10 \\ \hline 8 \end{array}$	23) $\begin{array}{r} 32 \\ -\ \boxed{} \\ \hline 22 \end{array}$	24) $\begin{array}{r} \boxed{} \\ -\ 35 \\ \hline 1 \end{array}$
25) $\begin{array}{r} 39 \\ -\ \boxed{} \\ \hline 10 \end{array}$	26) $\begin{array}{r} \boxed{} \\ -\ 19 \\ \hline 16 \end{array}$	27) $\begin{array}{r} 30 \\ -\ \boxed{} \\ \hline 7 \end{array}$	28) $\begin{array}{r} \boxed{} \\ -\ 14 \\ \hline 3 \end{array}$	29) $\begin{array}{r} 30 \\ -\ \boxed{} \\ \hline 7 \end{array}$	30) $\begin{array}{r} \boxed{} \\ -\ 25 \\ \hline 4 \end{array}$
31) $\begin{array}{r} 38 \\ -\ \boxed{} \\ \hline 17 \end{array}$	32) $\begin{array}{r} \boxed{} \\ -\ 15 \\ \hline 25 \end{array}$	33) $\begin{array}{r} 33 \\ -\ \boxed{} \\ \hline 21 \end{array}$	34) $\begin{array}{r} \boxed{} \\ -\ 31 \\ \hline 6 \end{array}$	35) $\begin{array}{r} 25 \\ -\ \boxed{} \\ \hline 14 \end{array}$	36) $\begin{array}{r} \boxed{} \\ -\ 25 \\ \hline 6 \end{array}$
37) $\begin{array}{r} 35 \\ -\ \boxed{} \\ \hline 12 \end{array}$	38) $\begin{array}{r} \boxed{} \\ -\ 14 \\ \hline 16 \end{array}$	39) $\begin{array}{r} 32 \\ -\ \boxed{} \\ \hline 0 \end{array}$	40) $\begin{array}{r} \boxed{} \\ -\ 23 \\ \hline 17 \end{array}$	41) $\begin{array}{r} 18 \\ -\ \boxed{} \\ \hline 1 \end{array}$	42) $\begin{array}{r} \boxed{} \\ -\ 18 \\ \hline 6 \end{array}$
43) $\begin{array}{r} 39 \\ -\ \boxed{} \\ \hline 1 \end{array}$	44) $\begin{array}{r} \boxed{} \\ -\ 15 \\ \hline 25 \end{array}$	45) $\begin{array}{r} 29 \\ -\ \boxed{} \\ \hline 17 \end{array}$	46) $\begin{array}{r} \boxed{} \\ -\ 10 \\ \hline 16 \end{array}$	47) $\begin{array}{r} 22 \\ -\ \boxed{} \\ \hline 1 \end{array}$	48) $\begin{array}{r} \boxed{} \\ -\ 17 \\ \hline 7 \end{array}$
49) $\begin{array}{r} 33 \\ -\ \boxed{} \\ \hline 4 \end{array}$	50) $\begin{array}{r} \boxed{} \\ -\ 34 \\ \hline 4 \end{array}$	51) $\begin{array}{r} 37 \\ -\ \boxed{} \\ \hline 19 \end{array}$	52) $\begin{array}{r} \boxed{} \\ -\ 10 \\ \hline 11 \end{array}$	53) $\begin{array}{r} 22 \\ -\ \boxed{} \\ \hline 10 \end{array}$	54) $\begin{array}{r} \boxed{} \\ -\ 17 \\ \hline 4 \end{array}$
55) $\begin{array}{r} 39 \\ -\ \boxed{} \\ \hline 11 \end{array}$	56) $\begin{array}{r} \boxed{} \\ -\ 29 \\ \hline 1 \end{array}$	57) $\begin{array}{r} 16 \\ -\ \boxed{} \\ \hline 2 \end{array}$	58) $\begin{array}{r} \boxed{} \\ -\ 13 \\ \hline 13 \end{array}$	59) $\begin{array}{r} 30 \\ -\ \boxed{} \\ \hline 4 \end{array}$	60) $\begin{array}{r} \boxed{} \\ -\ 17 \\ \hline 14 \end{array}$

1) 65 − 41

2) 56 − 51

3) 50 − 47

4) 43 − 40

5) 67 − 53

6) 56 − 56

7) 57 − 40

8) 60 − 58

9) 50 − 47

10) 46 − 46

11) 44 − 44

12) 66 − 44

13) 58 − 53

14) 58 − 40

15) 69 − 53

16) 57 − 50

17) 57 − 57

18) 59 − 46

19) 62 − 50

20) 64 − 61

21) 69 − 68

22) 52 − 43

23) 66 − 58

24) 52 − 41

25) 60 − 46

26) 61 − 56

27) 54 − 49

28) 55 − 45

29) 62 − 59

30) 57 − 44

31) 70 − 55

32) 69 − 42

33) 65 − 55

34) 69 − 50

35) 51 − 51

36) 58 − 43

37) 58 − 43

38) 62 − 40

39) 62 − 45

40) 56 − 45

41) 67 − 42

42) 50 − 47

43) 50 − 44

44) 64 − 46

45) 61 − 47

46) 68 − 65

47) 42 − 40

48) 63 − 41

49) 66 − 47

50) 45 − 45

51) 70 − 52

52) 48 − 41

53) 70 − 69

54) 52 − 47

55) 48 − 47

56) 62 − 58

57) 52 − 47

58) 55 − 53

59) 65 − 47

60) 54 − 46

1) 54 − 50

2) 69 − 60

3) 70 − 42

4) 62 − 41

5) 64 − 57

6) 58 − 46

7) 70 − 48

8) 65 − 53

9) 53 − 47

10) 49 − 43

11) 68 − 67

12) 63 − 58

13) 45 − 40

14) 60 − 58

15) 57 − 51

16) 64 − 64

17) 64 − 51

18) 67 − 55

19) 69 − 67

20) 62 − 44

21) 64 − 42

22) 61 − 61

23) 43 − 40

24) 55 − 54

25) 58 − 53

26) 56 − 48

27) 70 − 41

28) 58 − 53

29) 56 − 56

30) 53 − 47

31) 65 − 53

32) 51 − 45

33) 60 − 50

34) 52 − 47

35) 53 − 49

36) 51 − 51

37) 65 − 55

38) 62 − 46

39) 51 − 45

40) 48 − 47

41) 50 − 49

42) 60 − 56

43) 54 − 44

44) 69 − 44

45) 59 − 52

46) 55 − 51

47) 66 − 58

48) 70 − 63

49) 45 − 41

50) 63 − 58

51) 67 − 49

52) 53 − 50

53) 65 − 64

54) 59 − 53

55) 63 − 56

56) 49 − 44

57) 46 − 41

58) 59 − 40

59) 57 − 55

60) 43 − 41

1) 67 − 56

2) 60 − 53

3) 45 − 42

4) 53 − 53

5) 52 − 42

6) 51 − 48

7) 49 − 45

8) 57 − 40

9) 43 − 40

10) 50 − 41

11) 69 − 58

12) 60 − 51

13) 66 − 58

14) 63 − 59

15) 70 − 40

16) 45 − 41

17) 69 − 52

18) 49 − 48

19) 52 − 46

20) 53 − 52

21) 70 − 45

22) 70 − 58

23) 70 − 62

24) 61 − 59

25) 62 − 52

26) 66 − 55

27) 62 − 55

28) 54 − 51

29) 65 − 60

30) 65 − 40

31) 62 − 55

32) 67 − 65

33) 52 − 46

34) 56 − 44

35) 58 − 55

36) 45 − 42

37) 59 − 41

38) 57 − 54

39) 68 − 64

40) 50 − 46

41) 62 − 51

42) 54 − 53

43) 68 − 56

44) 46 − 42

45) 66 − 59

46) 66 − 61

47) 63 − 61

48) 64 − 58

49) 57 − 55

50) 54 − 40

51) 67 − 59

52) 68 − 67

53) 61 − 60

54) 55 − 51

55) 58 − 48

56) 64 − 42

57) 70 − 54

58) 51 − 45

59) 59 − 54

60) 46 − 44

Page 64

Time:

Subtracting Digits 40-70

Name:

Score

/60

1) $\begin{array}{r} 65 \\ -43 \end{array}$	2) $\begin{array}{r} 61 \\ -46 \end{array}$	3) $\begin{array}{r} 68 \\ -42 \end{array}$	4) $\begin{array}{r} 70 \\ -56 \end{array}$	5) $\begin{array}{r} 53 \\ -47 \end{array}$	6) $\begin{array}{r} 60 \\ -48 \end{array}$
7) $\begin{array}{r} 65 \\ -61 \end{array}$	8) $\begin{array}{r} 70 \\ -54 \end{array}$	9) $\begin{array}{r} 51 \\ -47 \end{array}$	10) $\begin{array}{r} 65 \\ -60 \end{array}$	11) $\begin{array}{r} 64 \\ -53 \end{array}$	12) $\begin{array}{r} 63 \\ -52 \end{array}$
13) $\begin{array}{r} 59 \\ -57 \end{array}$	14) $\begin{array}{r} 65 \\ -48 \end{array}$	15) $\begin{array}{r} 61 \\ -50 \end{array}$	16) $\begin{array}{r} 51 \\ -44 \end{array}$	17) $\begin{array}{r} 69 \\ -58 \end{array}$	18) $\begin{array}{r} 63 \\ -56 \end{array}$
19) $\begin{array}{r} 48 \\ -42 \end{array}$	20) $\begin{array}{r} 62 \\ -57 \end{array}$	21) $\begin{array}{r} 62 \\ -49 \end{array}$	22) $\begin{array}{r} 63 \\ -58 \end{array}$	23) $\begin{array}{r} 57 \\ -49 \end{array}$	24) $\begin{array}{r} 59 \\ -55 \end{array}$
25) $\begin{array}{r} 56 \\ -49 \end{array}$	26) $\begin{array}{r} 60 \\ -42 \end{array}$	27) $\begin{array}{r} 46 \\ -44 \end{array}$	28) $\begin{array}{r} 63 \\ -52 \end{array}$	29) $\begin{array}{r} 70 \\ -66 \end{array}$	30) $\begin{array}{r} 52 \\ -51 \end{array}$
31) $\begin{array}{r} 49 \\ -40 \end{array}$	32) $\begin{array}{r} 42 \\ -42 \end{array}$	33) $\begin{array}{r} 56 \\ -49 \end{array}$	34) $\begin{array}{r} 54 \\ -53 \end{array}$	35) $\begin{array}{r} 56 \\ -52 \end{array}$	36) $\begin{array}{r} 43 \\ -41 \end{array}$
37) $\begin{array}{r} 47 \\ -46 \end{array}$	38) $\begin{array}{r} 54 \\ -50 \end{array}$	39) $\begin{array}{r} 47 \\ -42 \end{array}$	40) $\begin{array}{r} 57 \\ -44 \end{array}$	41) $\begin{array}{r} 68 \\ -64 \end{array}$	42) $\begin{array}{r} 45 \\ -42 \end{array}$
43) $\begin{array}{r} 69 \\ -48 \end{array}$	44) $\begin{array}{r} 54 \\ -44 \end{array}$	45) $\begin{array}{r} 63 \\ -49 \end{array}$	46) $\begin{array}{r} 69 \\ -45 \end{array}$	47) $\begin{array}{r} 68 \\ -49 \end{array}$	48) $\begin{array}{r} 67 \\ -59 \end{array}$
49) $\begin{array}{r} 63 \\ -55 \end{array}$	50) $\begin{array}{r} 54 \\ -49 \end{array}$	51) $\begin{array}{r} 67 \\ -57 \end{array}$	52) $\begin{array}{r} 65 \\ -51 \end{array}$	53) $\begin{array}{r} 65 \\ -47 \end{array}$	54) $\begin{array}{r} 56 \\ -48 \end{array}$
55) $\begin{array}{r} 56 \\ -45 \end{array}$	56) $\begin{array}{r} 64 \\ -48 \end{array}$	57) $\begin{array}{r} 68 \\ -56 \end{array}$	58) $\begin{array}{r} 51 \\ -50 \end{array}$	59) $\begin{array}{r} 65 \\ -63 \end{array}$	60) $\begin{array}{r} 63 \\ -58 \end{array}$

1) 55 − 45

2) 44 − 41

3) 61 − 43

4) 58 − 42

5) 64 − 49

6) 66 − 61

7) 68 − 47

8) 50 − 45

9) 48 − 46

10) 52 − 41

11) 69 − 68

12) 57 − 50

13) 57 − 42

14) 56 − 50

15) 59 − 58

16) 61 − 48

17) 56 − 54

18) 61 − 54

19) 45 − 40

20) 69 − 54

21) 68 − 44

22) 64 − 49

23) 69 − 40

24) 68 − 58

25) 67 − 45

26) 61 − 51

27) 65 − 47

28) 58 − 49

29) 68 − 66

30) 57 − 45

31) 67 − 46

32) 68 − 53

33) 66 − 54

34) 65 − 59

35) 70 − 43

36) 66 − 46

37) 56 − 46

38) 66 − 40

39) 65 − 40

40) 61 − 46

41) 55 − 48

42) 67 − 45

43) 64 − 43

44) 70 − 59

45) 70 − 49

46) 62 − 43

47) 62 − 46

48) 66 − 62

49) 65 − 56

50) 66 − 57

51) 41 − 40

52) 68 − 64

53) 66 − 45

54) 45 − 45

55) 66 − 40

56) 68 − 68

57) 69 − 42

58) 64 − 49

59) 53 − 53

60) 65 − 57

Subtracting Digits 40-70

Name:

1) 58
  − ☐
   7

2) ☐
  − 70
   0

3) 61
  − ☐
   0

4) ☐
  − 47
  14

5) 52
  − ☐
   8

6) ☐
  − 43
   4

7) 62
  − ☐
   9

8) ☐
  − 61
   3

9) 52
  − ☐
   1

10) ☐
  − 49
  17

11) 67
  − ☐
  27

12) ☐
  − 50
   3

13) 59
  − ☐
   2

14) ☐
  − 50
  20

15) 64
  − ☐
   6

16) ☐
  − 44
  14

17) 58
  − ☐
   8

18) ☐
  − 55
   4

19) 67
  − ☐
  26

20) ☐
  − 40
   4

21) 54
  − ☐
   6

22) ☐
  − 45
   3

23) 57
  − ☐
  16

24) ☐
  − 53
  15

25) 69
  − ☐
   0

26) ☐
  − 44
   2

27) 64
  − ☐
   9

28) ☐
  − 44
  14

29) 48
  − ☐
   7

30) ☐
  − 48
  20

31) 63
  − ☐
  14

32) ☐
  − 45
  15

33) 65
  − ☐
  24

34) ☐
  − 58
  12

35) 61
  − ☐
   0

36) ☐
  − 54
  12

37) 59
  − ☐
   8

38) ☐
  − 47
  23

39) 67
  − ☐
   3

40) ☐
  − 40
  23

41) 68
  − ☐
   0

42) ☐
  − 40
   3

43) 51
  − ☐
   6

44) ☐
  − 52
   9

45) 55
  − ☐
   0

46) ☐
  − 51
   8

47) 59
  − ☐
   0

48) ☐
  − 44
  12

49) 67
  − ☐
  10

50) ☐
  − 54
  16

51) 64
  − ☐
  16

52) ☐
  − 48
  17

53) 60
  − ☐
   6

54) ☐
  − 51
  14

55) 68
  − ☐
  25

56) ☐
  − 56
   5

57) 65
  − ☐
  14

58) ☐
  − 60
   3

59) 47
  − ☐
   1

60) ☐
  − 40
  22

1) 67
  − ☐
  19

2) ☐
  − 46
  17

3) 60
  − ☐
  13

4) ☐
  − 40
  18

5) 63
  − ☐
  5

6) ☐
  − 45
  13

7) 68
  − ☐
  25

8) ☐
  − 45
  13

9) 49
  − ☐
  9

10) ☐
  − 41
  4

11) 62
  − ☐
  1

12) ☐
  − 51
  8

13) 58
  − ☐
  10

14) ☐
  − 40
  30

15) 56
  − ☐
  10

16) ☐
  − 44
  7

17) 69
  − ☐
  23

18) ☐
  − 49
  3

19) 66
  − ☐
  16

20) ☐
  − 45
  20

21) 47
  − ☐
  0

22) ☐
  − 42
  10

23) 65
  − ☐
  24

24) ☐
  − 56
  0

25) 68
  − ☐
  1

26) ☐
  − 42
  14

27) 65
  − ☐
  19

28) ☐
  − 41
  26

29) 69
  − ☐
  12

30) ☐
  − 47
  9

31) 62
  − ☐
  4

32) ☐
  − 53
  4

33) 70
  − ☐
  2

34) ☐
  − 40
  8

35) 65
  − ☐
  10

36) ☐
  − 43
  15

37) 48
  − ☐
  8

38) ☐
  − 43
  17

39) 70
  − ☐
  29

40) ☐
  − 62
  0

41) 70
  − ☐
  29

42) ☐
  − 49
  18

43) 46
  − ☐
  3

44) ☐
  − 62
  4

45) 59
  − ☐
  10

46) ☐
  − 47
  7

47) 68
  − ☐
  19

48) ☐
  − 42
  21

49) 44
  − ☐
  4

50) ☐
  − 46
  9

51) 47
  − ☐
  6

52) ☐
  − 49
  4

53) 69
  − ☐
  19

54) ☐
  − 41
  9

55) 58
  − ☐
  11

56) ☐
  − 68
  0

57) 52
  − ☐
  4

58) ☐
  − 47
  1

59) 61
  − ☐
  12

60) ☐
  − 54
  0

1)
```
   70
-  □
─────
   21
```

2)
```
   □
-  45
─────
   7
```

3)
```
   58
-  □
─────
   9
```

4)
```
   □
-  47
─────
   22
```

5)
```
   62
-  □
─────
   17
```

6)
```
   □
-  47
─────
   18
```

7)
```
   55
-  □
─────
   3
```

8)
```
   □
-  42
─────
   21
```

9)
```
   64
-  □
─────
   7
```

10)
```
   □
-  45
─────
   5
```

11)
```
   67
-  □
─────
   7
```

12)
```
   □
-  62
─────
   6
```

13)
```
   63
-  □
─────
   19
```

14)
```
   □
-  54
─────
   5
```

15)
```
   62
-  □
─────
   4
```

16)
```
   □
-  44
─────
   7
```

17)
```
   64
-  □
─────
   16
```

18)
```
   □
-  44
─────
   25
```

19)
```
   42
-  □
─────
   2
```

20)
```
   □
-  50
─────
   20
```

21)
```
   68
-  □
─────
   3
```

22)
```
   □
-  57
─────
   12
```

23)
```
   51
-  □
─────
   4
```

24)
```
   □
-  42
─────
   28
```

25)
```
   62
-  □
─────
   12
```

26)
```
   □
-  51
─────
   11
```

27)
```
   60
-  □
─────
   20
```

28)
```
   □
-  42
─────
   17
```

29)
```
   57
-  □
─────
   17
```

30)
```
   □
-  59
─────
   9
```

31)
```
   63
-  □
─────
   18
```

32)
```
   □
-  54
─────
   5
```

33)
```
   69
-  □
─────
   25
```

34)
```
   □
-  47
─────
   5
```

35)
```
   54
-  □
─────
   4
```

36)
```
   □
-  41
─────
   26
```

37)
```
   58
-  □
─────
   14
```

38)
```
   □
-  45
─────
   12
```

39)
```
   70
-  □
─────
   16
```

40)
```
   □
-  48
─────
   3
```

41)
```
   61
-  □
─────
   12
```

42)
```
   □
-  44
─────
   1
```

43)
```
   61
-  □
─────
   21
```

44)
```
   □
-  51
─────
   15
```

45)
```
   63
-  □
─────
   17
```

46)
```
   □
-  41
─────
   5
```

47)
```
   67
-  □
─────
   3
```

48)
```
   □
-  58
─────
   3
```

49)
```
   70
-  □
─────
   2
```

50)
```
   □
-  46
─────
   11
```

51)
```
   68
-  □
─────
   6
```

52)
```
   □
-  58
─────
   7
```

53)
```
   61
-  □
─────
   21
```

54)
```
   □
-  54
─────
   3
```

55)
```
   48
-  □
─────
   1
```

56)
```
   □
-  51
─────
   17
```

57)
```
   58
-  □
─────
   9
```

58)
```
   □
-  41
─────
   25
```

59)
```
   52
-  □
─────
   0
```

60)
```
   □
-  46
─────
   4
```

1)
```
   63
-  □
─────
    7
```

2)
```
   □
-  43
─────
   18
```

3)
```
   70
-  □
─────
    5
```

4)
```
   □
-  57
─────
    8
```

5)
```
   44
-  □
─────
    4
```

6)
```
   □
-  48
─────
    7
```

7)
```
   62
-  □
─────
    2
```

8)
```
   □
-  41
─────
   16
```

9)
```
   67
-  □
─────
   25
```

10)
```
   □
-  50
─────
   13
```

11)
```
   68
-  □
─────
   17
```

12)
```
   □
-  60
─────
    3
```

13)
```
   50
-  □
─────
    6
```

14)
```
   □
-  52
─────
   14
```

15)
```
   62
-  □
─────
    4
```

16)
```
   □
-  65
─────
    1
```

17)
```
   70
-  □
─────
   19
```

18)
```
   □
-  51
─────
    6
```

19)
```
   58
-  □
─────
   13
```

20)
```
   □
-  40
─────
    5
```

21)
```
   50
-  □
─────
    6
```

22)
```
   □
-  59
─────
    8
```

23)
```
   62
-  □
─────
   15
```

24)
```
   □
-  44
─────
   20
```

25)
```
   54
-  □
─────
    4
```

26)
```
   □
-  44
─────
   16
```

27)
```
   61
-  □
─────
   21
```

28)
```
   □
-  45
─────
    4
```

29)
```
   51
-  □
─────
    9
```

30)
```
   □
-  51
─────
    2
```

31)
```
   69
-  □
─────
   21
```

32)
```
   □
-  45
─────
   17
```

33)
```
   64
-  □
─────
   13
```

34)
```
   □
-  61
─────
    5
```

35)
```
   48
-  □
─────
    6
```

36)
```
   □
-  57
─────
   13
```

37)
```
   67
-  □
─────
    6
```

38)
```
   □
-  65
─────
    3
```

39)
```
   62
-  □
─────
   14
```

40)
```
   □
-  41
─────
   29
```

41)
```
   69
-  □
─────
    4
```

42)
```
   □
-  55
─────
    0
```

43)
```
   61
-  □
─────
    1
```

44)
```
   □
-  47
─────
   16
```

45)
```
   61
-  □
─────
   17
```

46)
```
   □
-  50
─────
    9
```

47)
```
   55
-  □
─────
   11
```

48)
```
   □
-  53
─────
    2
```

49)
```
   52
-  □
─────
    2
```

50)
```
   □
-  60
─────
    6
```

51)
```
   66
-  □
─────
   13
```

52)
```
   □
-  49
─────
   14
```

53)
```
   54
-  □
─────
    0
```

54)
```
   □
-  45
─────
   11
```

55)
```
   58
-  □
─────
   16
```

56)
```
   □
-  63
─────
    7
```

57)
```
   53
-  □
─────
   11
```

58)
```
   □
-  61
─────
    8
```

59)
```
   44
-  □
─────
    0
```

60)
```
   □
-  42
─────
   20
```

1)
$$\begin{array}{r} 49 \\ - \boxed{} \\ \hline 3 \end{array}$$

2)
$$\begin{array}{r} \boxed{} \\ - 46 \\ \hline 8 \end{array}$$

3)
$$\begin{array}{r} 59 \\ - \boxed{} \\ \hline 6 \end{array}$$

4)
$$\begin{array}{r} \boxed{} \\ - 43 \\ \hline 7 \end{array}$$

5)
$$\begin{array}{r} 49 \\ - \boxed{} \\ \hline 0 \end{array}$$

6)
$$\begin{array}{r} \boxed{} \\ - 57 \\ \hline 6 \end{array}$$

7)
$$\begin{array}{r} 45 \\ - \boxed{} \\ \hline 1 \end{array}$$

8)
$$\begin{array}{r} \boxed{} \\ - 52 \\ \hline 4 \end{array}$$

9)
$$\begin{array}{r} 62 \\ - \boxed{} \\ \hline 17 \end{array}$$

10)
$$\begin{array}{r} \boxed{} \\ - 45 \\ \hline 22 \end{array}$$

11)
$$\begin{array}{r} 69 \\ - \boxed{} \\ \hline 20 \end{array}$$

12)
$$\begin{array}{r} \boxed{} \\ - 58 \\ \hline 8 \end{array}$$

13)
$$\begin{array}{r} 63 \\ - \boxed{} \\ \hline 16 \end{array}$$

14)
$$\begin{array}{r} \boxed{} \\ - 42 \\ \hline 6 \end{array}$$

15)
$$\begin{array}{r} 55 \\ - \boxed{} \\ \hline 10 \end{array}$$

16)
$$\begin{array}{r} \boxed{} \\ - 42 \\ \hline 8 \end{array}$$

17)
$$\begin{array}{r} 70 \\ - \boxed{} \\ \hline 3 \end{array}$$

18)
$$\begin{array}{r} \boxed{} \\ - 42 \\ \hline 0 \end{array}$$

19)
$$\begin{array}{r} 69 \\ - \boxed{} \\ \hline 12 \end{array}$$

20)
$$\begin{array}{r} \boxed{} \\ - 70 \\ \hline 0 \end{array}$$

21)
$$\begin{array}{r} 59 \\ - \boxed{} \\ \hline 15 \end{array}$$

22)
$$\begin{array}{r} \boxed{} \\ - 51 \\ \hline 11 \end{array}$$

23)
$$\begin{array}{r} 49 \\ - \boxed{} \\ \hline 5 \end{array}$$

24)
$$\begin{array}{r} \boxed{} \\ - 41 \\ \hline 20 \end{array}$$

25)
$$\begin{array}{r} 66 \\ - \boxed{} \\ \hline 6 \end{array}$$

26)
$$\begin{array}{r} \boxed{} \\ - 49 \\ \hline 0 \end{array}$$

27)
$$\begin{array}{r} 70 \\ - \boxed{} \\ \hline 5 \end{array}$$

28)
$$\begin{array}{r} \boxed{} \\ - 64 \\ \hline 4 \end{array}$$

29)
$$\begin{array}{r} 62 \\ - \boxed{} \\ \hline 5 \end{array}$$

30)
$$\begin{array}{r} \boxed{} \\ - 61 \\ \hline 0 \end{array}$$

31)
$$\begin{array}{r} 66 \\ - \boxed{} \\ \hline 13 \end{array}$$

32)
$$\begin{array}{r} \boxed{} \\ - 47 \\ \hline 19 \end{array}$$

33)
$$\begin{array}{r} 46 \\ - \boxed{} \\ \hline 1 \end{array}$$

34)
$$\begin{array}{r} \boxed{} \\ - 48 \\ \hline 17 \end{array}$$

35)
$$\begin{array}{r} 61 \\ - \boxed{} \\ \hline 13 \end{array}$$

36)
$$\begin{array}{r} \boxed{} \\ - 51 \\ \hline 10 \end{array}$$

37)
$$\begin{array}{r} 48 \\ - \boxed{} \\ \hline 3 \end{array}$$

38)
$$\begin{array}{r} \boxed{} \\ - 43 \\ \hline 6 \end{array}$$

39)
$$\begin{array}{r} 67 \\ - \boxed{} \\ \hline 26 \end{array}$$

40)
$$\begin{array}{r} \boxed{} \\ - 51 \\ \hline 17 \end{array}$$

41)
$$\begin{array}{r} 68 \\ - \boxed{} \\ \hline 8 \end{array}$$

42)
$$\begin{array}{r} \boxed{} \\ - 46 \\ \hline 23 \end{array}$$

43)
$$\begin{array}{r} 58 \\ - \boxed{} \\ \hline 5 \end{array}$$

44)
$$\begin{array}{r} \boxed{} \\ - 41 \\ \hline 16 \end{array}$$

45)
$$\begin{array}{r} 55 \\ - \boxed{} \\ \hline 14 \end{array}$$

46)
$$\begin{array}{r} \boxed{} \\ - 48 \\ \hline 16 \end{array}$$

47)
$$\begin{array}{r} 64 \\ - \boxed{} \\ \hline 6 \end{array}$$

48)
$$\begin{array}{r} \boxed{} \\ - 42 \\ \hline 28 \end{array}$$

49)
$$\begin{array}{r} 65 \\ - \boxed{} \\ \hline 23 \end{array}$$

50)
$$\begin{array}{r} \boxed{} \\ - 46 \\ \hline 14 \end{array}$$

51)
$$\begin{array}{r} 67 \\ - \boxed{} \\ \hline 23 \end{array}$$

52)
$$\begin{array}{r} \boxed{} \\ - 48 \\ \hline 5 \end{array}$$

53)
$$\begin{array}{r} 66 \\ - \boxed{} \\ \hline 3 \end{array}$$

54)
$$\begin{array}{r} \boxed{} \\ - 44 \\ \hline 18 \end{array}$$

55)
$$\begin{array}{r} 66 \\ - \boxed{} \\ \hline 6 \end{array}$$

56)
$$\begin{array}{r} \boxed{} \\ - 59 \\ \hline 8 \end{array}$$

57)
$$\begin{array}{r} 69 \\ - \boxed{} \\ \hline 27 \end{array}$$

58)
$$\begin{array}{r} \boxed{} \\ - 40 \\ \hline 18 \end{array}$$

59)
$$\begin{array}{r} 60 \\ - \boxed{} \\ \hline 9 \end{array}$$

60)
$$\begin{array}{r} \boxed{} \\ - 56 \\ \hline 12 \end{array}$$

1) $93 - 92$

2) $70 - 70$

3) $75 - 73$

4) $83 - 74$

5) $86 - 70$

6) $100 - 80$

7) $92 - 87$

8) $92 - 84$

9) $92 - 86$

10) $96 - 96$

11) $91 - 85$

12) $97 - 75$

13) $83 - 74$

14) $99 - 70$

15) $75 - 74$

16) $97 - 80$

17) $99 - 89$

18) $85 - 82$

19) $93 - 83$

20) $96 - 81$

21) $72 - 72$

22) $91 - 78$

23) $88 - 79$

24) $96 - 78$

25) $79 - 76$

26) $91 - 70$

27) $96 - 82$

28) $91 - 72$

29) $95 - 76$

30) $94 - 87$

31) $96 - 95$

32) $88 - 86$

33) $94 - 72$

34) $92 - 72$

35) $87 - 80$

36) $90 - 74$

37) $97 - 79$

38) $96 - 78$

39) $81 - 81$

40) $96 - 92$

41) $82 - 78$

42) $97 - 79$

43) $87 - 83$

44) $99 - 80$

45) $79 - 73$

46) $98 - 90$

47) $93 - 79$

48) $86 - 81$

49) $87 - 86$

50) $89 - 74$

51) $93 - 73$

52) $90 - 72$

53) $99 - 96$

54) $92 - 89$

55) $83 - 83$

56) $85 - 71$

57) $95 - 94$

58) $91 - 81$

59) $93 - 93$

60) $100 - 95$

1) 93 − 90   2) 86 − 70   3) 95 − 75   4) 79 − 79   5) 78 − 77   6) 78 − 78

7) 96 − 95   8) 83 − 77   9) 78 − 74   10) 87 − 81   11) 87 − 71   12) 87 − 75

13) 81 − 74   14) 96 − 74   15) 98 − 86   16) 91 − 82   17) 96 − 70   18) 87 − 77

19) 81 − 74   20) 83 − 79   21) 95 − 82   22) 80 − 77   23) 100 − 73   24) 78 − 73

25) 96 − 93   26) 98 − 86   27) 100 − 92   28) 82 − 70   29) 94 − 86   30) 90 − 89

31) 81 − 74   32) 97 − 70   33) 92 − 75   34) 98 − 76   35) 89 − 87   36) 94 − 72

37) 81 − 74   38) 90 − 77   39) 100 − 78   40) 99 − 95   41) 99 − 90   42) 90 − 70

43) 92 − 78   44) 77 − 70   45) 96 − 76   46) 96 − 91   47) 98 − 81   48) 88 − 76

49) 84 − 79   50) 99 − 70   51) 95 − 76   52) 96 − 82   53) 88 − 74   54) 89 − 80

55) 89 − 75   56) 97 − 94   57) 78 − 74   58) 89 − 88   59) 79 − 78   60) 76 − 71

1)
$$\begin{array}{r} 75 \\ - 74 \\ \hline \end{array}$$

2)
$$\begin{array}{r} 98 \\ - 71 \\ \hline \end{array}$$

3)
$$\begin{array}{r} 98 \\ - 76 \\ \hline \end{array}$$

4)
$$\begin{array}{r} 77 \\ - 76 \\ \hline \end{array}$$

5)
$$\begin{array}{r} 95 \\ - 73 \\ \hline \end{array}$$

6)
$$\begin{array}{r} 84 \\ - 76 \\ \hline \end{array}$$

7)
$$\begin{array}{r} 98 \\ - 90 \\ \hline \end{array}$$

8)
$$\begin{array}{r} 94 \\ - 90 \\ \hline \end{array}$$

9)
$$\begin{array}{r} 100 \\ - 70 \\ \hline \end{array}$$

10)
$$\begin{array}{r} 94 \\ - 92 \\ \hline \end{array}$$

11)
$$\begin{array}{r} 86 \\ - 81 \\ \hline \end{array}$$

12)
$$\begin{array}{r} 98 \\ - 92 \\ \hline \end{array}$$

13)
$$\begin{array}{r} 98 \\ - 94 \\ \hline \end{array}$$

14)
$$\begin{array}{r} 93 \\ - 83 \\ \hline \end{array}$$

15)
$$\begin{array}{r} 72 \\ - 72 \\ \hline \end{array}$$

16)
$$\begin{array}{r} 96 \\ - 82 \\ \hline \end{array}$$

17)
$$\begin{array}{r} 76 \\ - 72 \\ \hline \end{array}$$

18)
$$\begin{array}{r} 92 \\ - 73 \\ \hline \end{array}$$

19)
$$\begin{array}{r} 88 \\ - 74 \\ \hline \end{array}$$

20)
$$\begin{array}{r} 88 \\ - 84 \\ \hline \end{array}$$

21)
$$\begin{array}{r} 91 \\ - 90 \\ \hline \end{array}$$

22)
$$\begin{array}{r} 90 \\ - 76 \\ \hline \end{array}$$

23)
$$\begin{array}{r} 99 \\ - 86 \\ \hline \end{array}$$

24)
$$\begin{array}{r} 99 \\ - 99 \\ \hline \end{array}$$

25)
$$\begin{array}{r} 86 \\ - 82 \\ \hline \end{array}$$

26)
$$\begin{array}{r} 94 \\ - 91 \\ \hline \end{array}$$

27)
$$\begin{array}{r} 77 \\ - 77 \\ \hline \end{array}$$

28)
$$\begin{array}{r} 87 \\ - 79 \\ \hline \end{array}$$

29)
$$\begin{array}{r} 83 \\ - 74 \\ \hline \end{array}$$

30)
$$\begin{array}{r} 98 \\ - 74 \\ \hline \end{array}$$

31)
$$\begin{array}{r} 99 \\ - 83 \\ \hline \end{array}$$

32)
$$\begin{array}{r} 98 \\ - 72 \\ \hline \end{array}$$

33)
$$\begin{array}{r} 88 \\ - 83 \\ \hline \end{array}$$

34)
$$\begin{array}{r} 98 \\ - 75 \\ \hline \end{array}$$

35)
$$\begin{array}{r} 91 \\ - 77 \\ \hline \end{array}$$

36)
$$\begin{array}{r} 95 \\ - 91 \\ \hline \end{array}$$

37)
$$\begin{array}{r} 96 \\ - 84 \\ \hline \end{array}$$

38)
$$\begin{array}{r} 88 \\ - 80 \\ \hline \end{array}$$

39)
$$\begin{array}{r} 93 \\ - 93 \\ \hline \end{array}$$

40)
$$\begin{array}{r} 100 \\ - 86 \\ \hline \end{array}$$

41)
$$\begin{array}{r} 92 \\ - 82 \\ \hline \end{array}$$

42)
$$\begin{array}{r} 79 \\ - 71 \\ \hline \end{array}$$

43)
$$\begin{array}{r} 89 \\ - 81 \\ \hline \end{array}$$

44)
$$\begin{array}{r} 95 \\ - 90 \\ \hline \end{array}$$

45)
$$\begin{array}{r} 77 \\ - 76 \\ \hline \end{array}$$

46)
$$\begin{array}{r} 97 \\ - 84 \\ \hline \end{array}$$

47)
$$\begin{array}{r} 94 \\ - 71 \\ \hline \end{array}$$

48)
$$\begin{array}{r} 79 \\ - 74 \\ \hline \end{array}$$

49)
$$\begin{array}{r} 83 \\ - 79 \\ \hline \end{array}$$

50)
$$\begin{array}{r} 93 \\ - 75 \\ \hline \end{array}$$

51)
$$\begin{array}{r} 97 \\ - 73 \\ \hline \end{array}$$

52)
$$\begin{array}{r} 96 \\ - 89 \\ \hline \end{array}$$

53)
$$\begin{array}{r} 81 \\ - 78 \\ \hline \end{array}$$

54)
$$\begin{array}{r} 94 \\ - 91 \\ \hline \end{array}$$

55)
$$\begin{array}{r} 79 \\ - 76 \\ \hline \end{array}$$

56)
$$\begin{array}{r} 84 \\ - 79 \\ \hline \end{array}$$

57)
$$\begin{array}{r} 92 \\ - 86 \\ \hline \end{array}$$

58)
$$\begin{array}{r} 90 \\ - 87 \\ \hline \end{array}$$

59)
$$\begin{array}{r} 88 \\ - 74 \\ \hline \end{array}$$

60)
$$\begin{array}{r} 93 \\ - 93 \\ \hline \end{array}$$

1) 90 − 77	2) 93 − 86	3) 85 − 72	4) 98 − 82	5) 94 − 92	6) 95 − 89
7) 88 − 82	8) 99 − 90	9) 87 − 84	10) 99 − 94	11) 100 − 96	12) 98 − 98
13) 91 − 78	14) 96 − 73	15) 97 − 75	16) 87 − 84	17) 86 − 82	18) 99 − 98
19) 83 − 71	20) 94 − 87	21) 87 − 87	22) 83 − 80	23) 88 − 83	24) 88 − 88
25) 91 − 80	26) 93 − 90	27) 84 − 79	28) 79 − 71	29) 100 − 96	30) 89 − 81
31) 79 − 70	32) 96 − 90	33) 100 − 83	34) 87 − 78	35) 96 − 83	36) 93 − 86
37) 97 − 84	38) 100 − 71	39) 100 − 78	40) 85 − 81	41) 92 − 79	42) 75 − 71
43) 86 − 76	44) 85 − 76	45) 82 − 78	46) 96 − 94	47) 96 − 96	48) 83 − 75
49) 80 − 77	50) 99 − 91	51) 97 − 97	52) 95 − 82	53) 90 − 71	54) 86 − 84
55) 89 − 81	56) 85 − 72	57) 89 − 72	58) 97 − 83	59) 91 − 70	60) 90 − 86

1) 82 − 77

2) 90 − 74

3) 91 − 91

4) 94 − 93

5) 93 − 70

6) 97 − 77

7) 81 − 72

8) 95 − 70

9) 87 − 74

10) 88 − 88

11) 89 − 86

12) 99 − 72

13) 85 − 83

14) 78 − 73

15) 89 − 80

16) 89 − 89

17) 90 − 90

18) 91 − 81

19) 77 − 75

20) 91 − 79

21) 98 − 70

22) 97 − 80

23) 100 − 74

24) 92 − 74

25) 96 − 90

26) 93 − 81

27) 74 − 71

28) 100 − 93

29) 97 − 81

30) 71 − 71

31) 99 − 95

32) 81 − 81

33) 99 − 95

34) 91 − 73

35) 97 − 78

36) 86 − 70

37) 92 − 73

38) 88 − 85

39) 90 − 77

40) 100 − 77

41) 76 − 73

42) 83 − 75

43) 98 − 96

44) 97 − 89

45) 75 − 72

46) 89 − 85

47) 92 − 73

48) 85 − 79

49) 86 − 70

50) 85 − 76

51) 96 − 70

52) 79 − 72

53) 93 − 75

54) 94 − 94

55) 99 − 72

56) 72 − 71

57) 92 − 83

58) 91 − 77

59) 97 − 82

60) 94 − 92

1) 80 − □ = 5

2) □ − 80 = 5

3) 97 − □ = 16

4) □ − 73 = 0

5) 88 − □ = 0

6) □ − 78 = 12

7) 74 − □ = 3

8) □ − 79 = 16

9) 85 − □ = 10

10) □ − 84 = 7

11) 99 − □ = 5

12) □ − 78 = 4

13) 77 − □ = 6

14) □ − 78 = 11

15) 94 − □ = 2

16) □ − 97 = 3

17) 80 − □ = 7

18) □ − 98 = 1

19) 100 − □ = 5

20) □ − 73 = 11

21) 79 − □ = 8

22) □ − 86 = 6

23) 83 − □ = 5

24) □ − 79 = 15

25) 97 − □ = 6

26) □ − 75 = 21

27) 92 − □ = 15

28) □ − 83 = 7

29) 95 − □ = 5

30) □ − 73 = 14

31) 85 − □ = 13

32) □ − 91 = 5

33) 86 − □ = 12

34) □ − 81 = 18

35) 82 − □ = 12

36) □ − 88 = 3

37) 94 − □ = 20

38) □ − 71 = 5

39) 82 − □ = 10

40) □ − 70 = 6

41) 98 − □ = 14

42) □ − 72 = 15

43) 83 − □ = 3

44) □ − 78 = 14

45) 98 − □ = 0

46) □ − 83 = 5

47) 96 − □ = 4

48) □ − 71 = 8

49) 91 − □ = 18

50) □ − 82 = 8

51) 99 − □ = 4

52) □ − 82 = 2

53) 86 − □ = 8

54) □ − 79 = 2

55) 92 − □ = 2

56) □ − 80 = 13

57) 89 − □ = 2

58) □ − 73 = 15

59) 100 − □ = 21

60) □ − 82 = 13

Score /60   Name: Time:

1) $\quad$ 92 $-$ □ $=$ 11	2) $\quad$ □ $-$ 72 $=$ 0	3) $\quad$ 97 $-$ □ $=$ 24
4) $\quad$ □ $-$ 71 $=$ 3	5) $\quad$ 91 $-$ □ $=$ 18	6) $\quad$ □ $-$ 78 $=$ 3
7) $\quad$ 79 $-$ □ $=$ 5	8) $\quad$ □ $-$ 79 $=$ 11	9) $\quad$ 92 $-$ □ $=$ 2
10) $\quad$ □ $-$ 71 $=$ 12	11) $\quad$ 99 $-$ □ $=$ 1	12) $\quad$ □ $-$ 73 $=$ 16
13) $\quad$ 96 $-$ □ $=$ 2	14) $\quad$ □ $-$ 86 $=$ 5	15) $\quad$ 93 $-$ □ $=$ 1
16) $\quad$ □ $-$ 90 $=$ 1	17) $\quad$ 89 $-$ □ $=$ 11	18) $\quad$ □ $-$ 72 $=$ 26
19) $\quad$ 100 $-$ □ $=$ 19	20) $\quad$ □ $-$ 72 $=$ 27	21) $\quad$ 95 $-$ □ $=$ 2
22) $\quad$ □ $-$ 98 $=$ 1	23) $\quad$ 88 $-$ □ $=$ 3	24) $\quad$ □ $-$ 95 $=$ 5
25) $\quad$ 98 $-$ □ $=$ 22	26) $\quad$ □ $-$ 74 $=$ 6	27) $\quad$ 100 $-$ □ $=$ 9
28) $\quad$ □ $-$ 76 $=$ 5	29) $\quad$ 95 $-$ □ $=$ 6	30) $\quad$ □ $-$ 86 $=$ 6
31) $\quad$ 90 $-$ □ $=$ 4	32) $\quad$ □ $-$ 73 $=$ 26	33) $\quad$ 75 $-$ □ $=$ 1
34) $\quad$ □ $-$ 77 $=$ 5	35) $\quad$ 95 $-$ □ $=$ 12	36) $\quad$ □ $-$ 72 $=$ 2
37) $\quad$ 84 $-$ □ $=$ 1	38) $\quad$ □ $-$ 76 $=$ 6	39) $\quad$ 86 $-$ □ $=$ 3
40) $\quad$ □ $-$ 76 $=$ 14	41) $\quad$ 80 $-$ □ $=$ 6	42) $\quad$ □ $-$ 74 $=$ 12
43) $\quad$ 84 $-$ □ $=$ 1	44) $\quad$ □ $-$ 82 $=$ 10	45) $\quad$ 79 $-$ □ $=$ 7
46) $\quad$ □ $-$ 76 $=$ 1	47) $\quad$ 91 $-$ □ $=$ 18	48) $\quad$ □ $-$ 79 $=$ 9
49) $\quad$ 96 $-$ □ $=$ 17	50) $\quad$ □ $-$ 92 $=$ 4	51) $\quad$ 82 $-$ □ $=$ 10
52) $\quad$ □ $-$ 100 $=$ 0	53) $\quad$ 91 $-$ □ $=$ 21	54) $\quad$ □ $-$ 74 $=$ 3
55) $\quad$ 97 $-$ □ $=$ 3	56) $\quad$ □ $-$ 71 $=$ 19	57) $\quad$ 89 $-$ □ $=$ 19
58) $\quad$ □ $-$ 82 $=$ 12	59) $\quad$ 80 $-$ □ $=$ 1	60) $\quad$ □ $-$ 93 $=$ 4

1) 85
   − ☐
   ─────
     9

2) ☐
   − 83
   ─────
    14

3) 90
   − ☐
   ─────
     3

4) ☐
   − 74
   ─────
    15

5) 91
   − ☐
   ─────
    14

6) ☐
   − 78
   ─────
    20

7) 79
   − ☐
   ─────
     8

8) ☐
   − 85
   ─────
     8

9) 89
   − ☐
   ─────
    17

10) ☐
   − 72
   ─────
    19

11) 87
   − ☐
   ─────
    10

12) ☐
   − 85
   ─────
     2

13) 100
   − ☐
   ─────
     4

14) ☐
   − 83
   ─────
     5

15) 79
   − ☐
   ─────
     4

16) ☐
   − 73
   ─────
     7

17) 84
   − ☐
   ─────
    13

18) ☐
   − 71
   ─────
     7

19) 93
   − ☐
   ─────
    13

20) ☐
   − 78
   ─────
    22

21) 91
   − ☐
   ─────
    10

22) ☐
   − 78
   ─────
    19

23) 81
   − ☐
   ─────
     2

24) ☐
   − 90
   ─────
     6

25) 76
   − ☐
   ─────
     6

26) ☐
   − 73
   ─────
    10

27) 99
   − ☐
   ─────
     2

28) ☐
   − 81
   ─────
     0

29) 95
   − ☐
   ─────
    12

30) ☐
   − 78
   ─────
    14

31) 98
   − ☐
   ─────
     0

32) ☐
   − 76
   ─────
     7

33) 81
   − ☐
   ─────
     0

34) ☐
   − 83
   ─────
    15

35) 93
   − ☐
   ─────
     1

36) ☐
   − 85
   ─────
     9

37) 85
   − ☐
   ─────
     0

38) ☐
   − 77
   ─────
     6

39) 99
   − ☐
   ─────
    17

40) ☐
   − 73
   ─────
    13

41) 77
   − ☐
   ─────
     1

42) ☐
   − 72
   ─────
    15

43) 74
   − ☐
   ─────
     0

44) ☐
   − 77
   ─────
    21

45) 91
   − ☐
   ─────
    15

46) ☐
   − 75
   ─────
     5

47) 89
   − ☐
   ─────
     2

48) ☐
   − 94
   ─────
     3

49) 90
   − ☐
   ─────
    11

50) ☐
   − 81
   ─────
    13

51) 100
   − ☐
   ─────
    25

52) ☐
   − 80
   ─────
    18

53) 84
   − ☐
   ─────
    12

54) ☐
   − 77
   ─────
    19

55) 94
   − ☐
   ─────
    19

56) ☐
   − 88
   ─────
    10

57) 100
   − ☐
   ─────
     0

58) ☐
   − 71
   ─────
     8

59) 100
   − ☐
   ─────
     6

60) ☐
   − 85
   ─────
    12

1) 78 − ☐ = 0

2) ☐ − 77 = 1

3) 96 − ☐ = 15

4) ☐ − 75 = 23

5) 86 − ☐ = 4

6) ☐ − 87 = 1

7) 88 − ☐ = 2

8) ☐ − 81 = 16

9) 90 − ☐ = 17

10) ☐ − 75 = 7

11) 87 − ☐ = 7

12) ☐ − 96 = 4

13) 99 − ☐ = 26

14) ☐ − 79 = 13

15) 85 − ☐ = 2

16) ☐ − 85 = 7

17) 90 − ☐ = 20

18) ☐ − 83 = 9

19) 89 − ☐ = 11

20) ☐ − 73 = 20

21) 93 − ☐ = 14

22) ☐ − 89 = 3

23) 90 − ☐ = 11

24) ☐ − 89 = 0

25) 93 − ☐ = 23

26) ☐ − 76 = 20

27) 84 − ☐ = 0

28) ☐ − 80 = 17

29) 96 − ☐ = 10

30) ☐ − 73 = 23

31) 93 − ☐ = 13

32) ☐ − 82 = 9

33) 80 − ☐ = 3

34) ☐ − 78 = 9

35) 99 − ☐ = 28

36) ☐ − 90 = 4

37) 92 − ☐ = 2

38) ☐ − 89 = 6

39) 80 − ☐ = 0

40) ☐ − 82 = 1

41) 85 − ☐ = 2

42) ☐ − 80 = 14

43) 83 − ☐ = 7

44) ☐ − 78 = 21

45) 81 − ☐ = 8

46) ☐ − 70 = 28

47) 83 − ☐ = 7

48) ☐ − 90 = 0

49) 76 − ☐ = 6

50) ☐ − 79 = 13

51) 82 − ☐ = 6

52) ☐ − 71 = 16

53) 100 − ☐ = 25

54) ☐ − 73 = 12

55) 74 − ☐ = 3

56) ☐ − 94 = 1

57) 90 − ☐ = 10

58) ☐ − 77 = 1

59) 93 − ☐ = 22

60) ☐ − 80 = 10

1) 81 − ☐ = 7
2) ☐ − 74 = 6
3) 89 − ☐ = 3
4) ☐ − 70 = 10
5) 97 − ☐ = 2
6) ☐ − 79 = 20

7) 94 − ☐ = 1
8) ☐ − 86 = 2
9) 87 − ☐ = 6
10) ☐ − 71 = 22
11) 100 − ☐ = 6
12) ☐ − 90 = 2

13) 93 − ☐ = 12
14) ☐ − 85 = 1
15) 99 − ☐ = 18
16) ☐ − 74 = 17
17) 81 − ☐ = 0
18) ☐ − 89 = 11

19) 91 − ☐ = 20
20) ☐ − 71 = 8
21) 89 − ☐ = 4
22) ☐ − 82 = 2
23) 98 − ☐ = 20
24) ☐ − 84 = 15

25) 95 − ☐ = 20
26) ☐ − 97 = 1
27) 90 − ☐ = 17
28) ☐ − 88 = 11
29) 84 − ☐ = 7
30) ☐ − 88 = 6

31) 95 − ☐ = 19
32) ☐ − 96 = 0
33) 100 − ☐ = 20
34) ☐ − 72 = 20
35) 90 − ☐ = 17
36) ☐ − 97 = 0

37) 76 − ☐ = 2
38) ☐ − 84 = 11
39) 97 − ☐ = 27
40) ☐ − 74 = 3
41) 87 − ☐ = 8
42) ☐ − 81 = 1

43) 88 − ☐ = 3
44) ☐ − 75 = 8
45) 94 − ☐ = 22
46) ☐ − 83 = 10
47) 84 − ☐ = 8
48) ☐ − 84 = 7

49) 82 − ☐ = 4
50) ☐ − 95 = 1
51) 98 − ☐ = 22
52) ☐ − 82 = 12
53) 99 − ☐ = 29
54) ☐ − 85 = 14

55) 83 − ☐ = 6
56) ☐ − 81 = 11
57) 100 − ☐ = 12
58) ☐ − 87 = 5
59) 99 − ☐ = 27
60) ☐ − 81 = 14

1) 127 − 108

2) 121 − 108

3) 121 − 117

4) 120 − 116

5) 126 − 112

6) 126 − 112

7) 114 − 101

8) 104 − 100

9) 129 − 107

10) 118 − 102

11) 128 − 111

12) 114 − 109

13) 121 − 100

14) 124 − 119

15) 129 − 110

16) 116 − 116

17) 129 − 104

18) 130 − 111

19) 115 − 100

20) 123 − 113

21) 126 − 104

22) 108 − 105

23) 123 − 120

24) 123 − 102

25) 130 − 119

26) 124 − 104

27) 125 − 102

28) 109 − 108

29) 114 − 101

30) 128 − 116

31) 116 − 110

32) 120 − 103

33) 130 − 122

34) 112 − 111

35) 107 − 107

36) 129 − 114

37) 122 − 101

38) 114 − 103

39) 125 − 119

40) 124 − 110

41) 121 − 110

42) 130 − 119

43) 127 − 118

44) 125 − 101

45) 115 − 108

46) 123 − 109

47) 121 − 117

48) 109 − 104

49) 116 − 104

50) 126 − 100

51) 129 − 103

52) 123 − 123

53) 116 − 110

54) 120 − 103

55) 129 − 105

56) 126 − 118

57) 123 − 115

58) 130 − 123

59) 114 − 110

60) 111 − 103

1) 130
  − 125

2) 118
  − 110

3) 117
  − 111

4) 108
  − 106

5) 123
  − 122

6) 122
  − 113

7) 119
  − 109

8) 127
  − 104

9) 107
  − 100

10) 117
  − 110

11) 109
  − 108

12) 124
  − 124

13) 103
  − 101

14) 115
  − 115

15) 119
  − 104

16) 129
  − 108

17) 114
  − 114

18) 117
  − 104

19) 129
  − 109

20) 115
  − 105

21) 127
  − 115

22) 126
  − 115

23) 129
  − 122

24) 114
  − 106

25) 119
  − 115

26) 121
  − 100

27) 127
  − 110

28) 109
  − 106

29) 129
  − 102

30) 120
  − 110

31) 113
  − 102

32) 116
  − 116

33) 118
  − 103

34) 121
  − 100

35) 106
  − 104

36) 110
  − 109

37) 118
  − 103

38) 117
  − 115

39) 106
  − 101

40) 130
  − 111

41) 123
  − 102

42) 109
  − 108

43) 127
  − 113

44) 126
  − 102

45) 115
  − 115

46) 120
  − 120

47) 130
  − 120

48) 126
  − 104

49) 115
  − 112

50) 114
  − 109

51) 117
  − 109

52) 124
  − 115

53) 119
  − 112

54) 128
  − 122

55) 108
  − 103

56) 127
  − 113

57) 107
  − 100

58) 107
  − 106

59) 122
  − 107

60) 120
  − 100

1) 116 − 101

2) 116 − 100

3) 124 − 119

4) 122 − 115

5) 128 − 118

6) 117 − 108

7) 110 − 108

8) 114 − 112

9) 126 − 123

10) 130 − 119

11) 126 − 107

12) 126 − 103

13) 108 − 102

14) 122 − 103

15) 127 − 121

16) 111 − 107

17) 115 − 100

18) 121 − 108

19) 128 − 121

20) 130 − 128

21) 129 − 118

22) 115 − 108

23) 100 − 100

24) 115 − 106

25) 128 − 100

26) 130 − 107

27) 128 − 102

28) 114 − 103

29) 112 − 107

30) 117 − 104

31) 117 − 110

32) 118 − 114

33) 120 − 118

34) 123 − 120

35) 112 − 112

36) 119 − 113

37) 121 − 120

38) 129 − 110

39) 125 − 118

40) 110 − 105

41) 118 − 118

42) 128 − 121

43) 125 − 113

44) 109 − 101

45) 114 − 112

46) 125 − 119

47) 122 − 120

48) 113 − 104

49) 127 − 119

50) 116 − 102

51) 125 − 116

52) 122 − 116

53) 107 − 100

54) 128 − 126

55) 129 − 110

56) 128 − 111

57) 126 − 111

58) 121 − 109

59) 124 − 124

60) 130 − 112

1) 127
  − 105

2) 115
  − 114

3) 115
  − 105

4) 125
  − 117

5) 130
  − 124

6) 120
  − 101

7) 110
  − 109

8) 116
  − 107

9) 125
  − 121

10) 118
  − 109

11) 129
  − 111

12) 123
  − 118

13) 128
  − 115

14) 102
  − 102

15) 120
  − 106

16) 126
  − 121

17) 130
  − 110

18) 121
  − 119

19) 119
  − 110

20) 109
  − 103

21) 128
  − 105

22) 130
  − 120

23) 102
  − 100

24) 107
  − 104

25) 115
  − 105

26) 129
  − 117

27) 114
  − 114

28) 119
  − 119

29) 114
  − 100

30) 124
  − 121

31) 127
  − 114

32) 126
  − 120

33) 126
  − 121

34) 126
  − 105

35) 106
  − 104

36) 126
  − 111

37) 125
  − 103

38) 125
  − 104

39) 109
  − 103

40) 120
  − 115

41) 120
  − 106

42) 127
  − 112

43) 113
  − 107

44) 114
  − 113

45) 128
  − 117

46) 118
  − 107

47) 126
  − 124

48) 125
  − 111

49) 117
  − 117

50) 118
  − 104

51) 130
  − 110

52) 126
  − 126

53) 129
  − 126

54) 122
  − 108

55) 106
  − 103

56) 110
  − 102

57) 126
  − 116

58) 125
  − 106

59) 123
  − 107

60) 130
  − 130

1) 130 − 100
2) 123 − 115
3) 130 − 106
4) 112 − 111
5) 126 − 120
6) 108 − 105

7) 128 − 128
8) 130 − 130
9) 107 − 104
10) 111 − 111
11) 128 − 111
12) 128 − 116

13) 127 − 127
14) 127 − 118
15) 127 − 115
16) 118 − 116
17) 113 − 112
18) 128 − 126

19) 110 − 104
20) 105 − 105
21) 125 − 124
22) 110 − 101
23) 119 − 116
24) 122 − 107

25) 126 − 113
26) 119 − 110
27) 121 − 104
28) 130 − 112
29) 118 − 101
30) 126 − 111

31) 122 − 105
32) 119 − 113
33) 124 − 114
34) 124 − 118
35) 129 − 114
36) 125 − 109

37) 121 − 111
38) 125 − 115
39) 127 − 127
40) 127 − 125
41) 108 − 103
42) 123 − 119

43) 123 − 105
44) 115 − 104
45) 130 − 103
46) 129 − 100
47) 111 − 110
48) 123 − 120

49) 130 − 116
50) 121 − 102
51) 111 − 111
52) 128 − 127
53) 127 − 123
54) 123 − 104

55) 124 − 104
56) 122 − 116
57) 120 − 106
58) 128 − 110
59) 104 − 104
60) 122 − 110

1) 111
− ☐
3

2) ☐
− 106
5

3) 100
− ☐
0

4) ☐
− 108
13

5) 118
− ☐
15

6) ☐
− 101
10

7) 120
− ☐
7

8) ☐
− 109
5

9) 125
− ☐
12

10) ☐
− 116
14

11) 121
− ☐
11

12) ☐
− 106
24

13) 104
− ☐
2

14) ☐
− 104
1

15) 120
− ☐
6

16) ☐
− 121
1

17) 127
− ☐
27

18) ☐
− 116
3

19) 122
− ☐
2

20) ☐
− 112
2

21) 114
− ☐
2

22) ☐
− 114
2

23) 119
− ☐
13

24) ☐
− 118
9

25) 126
− ☐
18

26) ☐
− 125
1

27) 122
− ☐
7

28) ☐
− 120
1

29) 129
− ☐
21

30) ☐
− 100
8

31) 118
− ☐
13

32) ☐
− 107
14

33) 126
− ☐
19

34) ☐
− 103
3

35) 111
− ☐
10

36) ☐
− 120
8

37) 122
− ☐
1

38) ☐
− 110
3

39) 106
− ☐
6

40) ☐
− 104
8

41) 110
− ☐
6

42) ☐
− 103
3

43) 125
− ☐
4

44) ☐
− 100
18

45) 126
− ☐
25

46) ☐
− 105
18

47) 127
− ☐
5

48) ☐
− 109
15

49) 116
− ☐
11

50) ☐
− 114
15

51) 126
− ☐
10

52) ☐
− 119
7

53) 127
− ☐
0

54) ☐
− 103
7

55) 125
− ☐
23

56) ☐
− 103
8

57) 119
− ☐
8

58) ☐
− 105
18

59) 123
− ☐
23

60) ☐
− 100
17

1) 125
  − ☐
  11

2) ☐
  − 114
  8

3) 123
  − ☐
  17

4) ☐
  − 115
  5

5) 114
  − ☐
  0

6) ☐
  − 112
  3

7) 118
  − ☐
  10

8) ☐
  − 116
  9

9) 121
  − ☐
  17

10) ☐
  − 100
  23

11) 130
  − ☐
  4

12) ☐
  − 108
  7

13) 128
  − ☐
  28

14) ☐
  − 101
  23

15) 118
  − ☐
  7

16) ☐
  − 108
  14

17) 129
  − ☐
  3

18) ☐
  − 123
  3

19) 127
  − ☐
  17

20) ☐
  − 123
  6

21) 101
  − ☐
  0

22) ☐
  − 100
  11

23) 118
  − ☐
  5

24) ☐
  − 106
  15

25) 122
  − ☐
  21

26) ☐
  − 100
  16

27) 129
  − ☐
  18

28) ☐
  − 116
  3

29) 129
  − ☐
  27

30) ☐
  − 120
  0

31) 127
  − ☐
  12

32) ☐
  − 109
  8

33) 123
  − ☐
  18

34) ☐
  − 106
  1

35) 111
  − ☐
  3

36) ☐
  − 119
  5

37) 130
  − ☐
  23

38) ☐
  − 126
  1

39) 127
  − ☐
  6

40) ☐
  − 123
  4

41) 129
  − ☐
  11

42) ☐
  − 117
  11

43) 123
  − ☐
  23

44) ☐
  − 104
  25

45) 127
  − ☐
  18

46) ☐
  − 104
  19

47) 124
  − ☐
  21

48) ☐
  − 106
  13

49) 107
  − ☐
  1

50) ☐
  − 109
  9

51) 126
  − ☐
  21

52) ☐
  − 105
  17

53) 113
  − ☐
  1

54) ☐
  − 120
  6

55) 110
  − ☐
  2

56) ☐
  − 109
  8

57) 117
  − ☐
  6

58) ☐
  − 123
  2

59) 127
  − ☐
  4

60) ☐
  − 107
  4

Page 88
Time:
Subtracting Digits 100-130
Name:
Score
/60

1) 113
    – ☐
    4

2) ☐
    – 106
    17

3) 127
    – ☐
    26

4) ☐
    – 107
    11

5) 119
    – ☐
    0

6) ☐
    – 111
    1

7) 106
    – ☐
    0

8) ☐
    – 102
    15

9) 114
    – ☐
    12

10) ☐
    – 108
    18

11) 127
    – ☐
    11

12) ☐
    – 101
    26

13) 130
    – ☐
    12

14) ☐
    – 112
    13

15) 109
    – ☐
    1

16) ☐
    – 119
    7

17) 117
    – ☐
    6

18) ☐
    – 123
    1

19) 121
    – ☐
    5

20) ☐
    – 123
    4

21) 115
    – ☐
    10

22) ☐
    – 105
    0

23) 120
    – ☐
    1

24) ☐
    – 104
    22

25) 122
    – ☐
    17

26) ☐
    – 128
    1

27) 120
    – ☐
    0

28) ☐
    – 107
    16

29) 104
    – ☐
    0

30) ☐
    – 101
    20

31) 108
    – ☐
    8

32) ☐
    – 104
    4

33) 116
    – ☐
    11

34) ☐
    – 118
    4

35) 130
    – ☐
    15

36) ☐
    – 106
    19

37) 130
    – ☐
    27

38) ☐
    – 109
    16

39) 119
    – ☐
    13

40) ☐
    – 100
    30

41) 127
    – ☐
    13

42) ☐
    – 110
    3

43) 104
    – ☐
    2

44) ☐
    – 108
    8

45) 120
    – ☐
    2

46) ☐
    – 128
    2

47) 122
    – ☐
    3

48) ☐
    – 101
    16

49) 130
    – ☐
    4

50) ☐
    – 119
    8

51) 125
    – ☐
    22

52) ☐
    – 124
    4

53) 118
    – ☐
    18

54) ☐
    – 115
    0

55) 109
    – ☐
    3

56) ☐
    – 113
    0

57) 113
    – ☐
    2

58) ☐
    – 113
    8

59) 121
    – ☐
    18

60) ☐
    – 105
    12

1) 127 − ☐ = 0

2) ☐ − 102 = 12

3) 120 − ☐ = 2

4) ☐ − 106 = 22

5) 127 − ☐ = 17

6) ☐ − 117 = 1

7) 123 − ☐ = 18

8) ☐ − 101 = 3

9) 111 − ☐ = 0

10) ☐ − 100 = 10

11) 118 − ☐ = 16

12) ☐ − 102 = 19

13) 127 − ☐ = 16

14) ☐ − 108 = 15

15) 108 − ☐ = 3

16) ☐ − 120 = 4

17) 122 − ☐ = 2

18) ☐ − 115 = 15

19) 114 − ☐ = 10

20) ☐ − 115 = 6

21) 128 − ☐ = 6

22) ☐ − 122 = 0

23) 118 − ☐ = 8

24) ☐ − 109 = 20

25) 113 − ☐ = 11

26) ☐ − 109 = 10

27) 121 − ☐ = 2

28) ☐ − 111 = 17

29) 126 − ☐ = 12

30) ☐ − 122 = 7

31) 108 − ☐ = 7

32) ☐ − 118 = 12

33) 127 − ☐ = 11

34) ☐ − 104 = 20

35) 104 − ☐ = 0

36) ☐ − 110 = 14

37) 130 − ☐ = 17

38) ☐ − 105 = 23

39) 112 − ☐ = 4

40) ☐ − 100 = 5

41) 126 − ☐ = 25

42) ☐ − 108 = 6

43) 126 − ☐ = 24

44) ☐ − 106 = 13

45) 122 − ☐ = 8

46) ☐ − 114 = 6

47) 117 − ☐ = 7

48) ☐ − 111 = 2

49) 122 − ☐ = 19

50) ☐ − 107 = 8

51) 126 − ☐ = 8

52) ☐ − 107 = 13

53) 124 − ☐ = 17

54) ☐ − 108 = 22

55) 111 − ☐ = 1

56) ☐ − 104 = 23

57) 115 − ☐ = 1

58) ☐ − 107 = 5

59) 130 − ☐ = 11

60) ☐ − 101 = 22

1) 129 − ☐ = 15

2) ☐ − 100 = 29

3) 127 − ☐ = 22

4) ☐ − 108 = 13

5) 122 − ☐ = 18

6) ☐ − 108 = 0

7) 127 − ☐ = 25

8) ☐ − 114 = 11

9) 129 − ☐ = 1

10) ☐ − 103 = 4

11) 125 − ☐ = 21

12) ☐ − 107 = 15

13) 108 − ☐ = 0

14) ☐ − 126 = 4

15) 117 − ☐ = 16

16) ☐ − 119 = 10

17) 108 − ☐ = 4

18) ☐ − 116 = 6

19) 130 − ☐ = 5

20) ☐ − 101 = 28

21) 130 − ☐ = 30

22) ☐ − 101 = 2

23) 126 − ☐ = 4

24) ☐ − 109 = 20

25) 128 − ☐ = 1

26) ☐ − 101 = 6

27) 122 − ☐ = 4

28) ☐ − 107 = 4

29) 110 − ☐ = 1

30) ☐ − 122 = 7

31) 113 − ☐ = 10

32) ☐ − 104 = 21

33) 120 − ☐ = 3

34) ☐ − 102 = 20

35) 116 − ☐ = 16

36) ☐ − 101 = 23

37) 127 − ☐ = 2

38) ☐ − 100 = 10

39) 113 − ☐ = 4

40) ☐ − 101 = 22

41) 117 − ☐ = 13

42) ☐ − 112 = 10

43) 125 − ☐ = 13

44) ☐ − 105 = 21

45) 119 − ☐ = 15

46) ☐ − 108 = 7

47) 107 − ☐ = 4

48) ☐ − 104 = 22

49) 121 − ☐ = 16

50) ☐ − 118 = 10

51) 112 − ☐ = 7

52) ☐ − 104 = 14

53) 130 − ☐ = 20

54) ☐ − 114 = 14

55) 118 − ☐ = 18

56) ☐ − 107 = 7

57) 120 − ☐ = 5

58) ☐ − 113 = 6

59) 126 − ☐ = 11

60) ☐ − 105 = 25

1) 154 − 151
2) 139 − 138
3) 152 − 150
4) 150 − 149
5) 157 − 133
6) 136 − 133

7) 157 − 139
8) 154 − 133
9) 160 − 136
10) 147 − 135
11) 146 − 136
12) 149 − 130

13) 148 − 144
14) 142 − 141
15) 151 − 148
16) 140 − 130
17) 145 − 131
18) 134 − 130

19) 140 − 137
20) 146 − 136
21) 146 − 131
22) 154 − 140
23) 160 − 135
24) 156 − 148

25) 148 − 133
26) 145 − 142
27) 143 − 138
28) 151 − 137
29) 154 − 132
30) 148 − 138

31) 159 − 157
32) 158 − 151
33) 157 − 143
34) 159 − 159
35) 148 − 132
36) 148 − 130

37) 131 − 130
38) 139 − 134
39) 152 − 147
40) 160 − 139
41) 155 − 148
42) 158 − 158

43) 140 − 137
44) 147 − 143
45) 146 − 136
46) 159 − 153
47) 131 − 131
48) 145 − 143

49) 154 − 142
50) 159 − 147
51) 147 − 138
52) 144 − 137
53) 151 − 138
54) 159 − 159

55) 142 − 136
56) 150 − 131
57) 146 − 138
58) 149 − 145
59) 153 − 144
60) 158 − 132

1) 154 − 135

2) 156 − 130

3) 141 − 132

4) 152 − 134

5) 150 − 143

6) 135 − 132

7) 151 − 131

8) 153 − 144

9) 145 − 132

10) 143 − 141

11) 155 − 149

12) 147 − 138

13) 142 − 131

14) 160 − 132

15) 158 − 152

16) 158 − 153

17) 154 − 139

18) 143 − 142

19) 145 − 144

20) 147 − 140

21) 141 − 136

22) 134 − 134

23) 146 − 140

24) 149 − 146

25) 159 − 158

26) 148 − 145

27) 157 − 146

28) 155 − 134

29) 150 − 142

30) 156 − 143

31) 142 − 131

32) 153 − 132

33) 159 − 155

34) 152 − 146

35) 144 − 131

36) 138 − 133

37) 146 − 133

38) 138 − 137

39) 154 − 150

40) 151 − 134

41) 140 − 130

42) 150 − 150

43) 160 − 144

44) 138 − 135

45) 145 − 135

46) 156 − 150

47) 155 − 155

48) 139 − 130

49) 149 − 137

50) 156 − 133

51) 160 − 140

52) 141 − 135

53) 150 − 139

54) 153 − 145

55) 146 − 131

56) 154 − 152

57) 146 − 132

58) 150 − 135

59) 159 − 144

60) 138 − 130

1) 138 − 131

2) 159 − 143

3) 151 − 132

4) 158 − 134

5) 151 − 138

6) 153 − 138

7) 143 − 140

8) 141 − 137

9) 152 − 136

10) 144 − 135

11) 157 − 155

12) 160 − 140

13) 150 − 142

14) 149 − 144

15) 150 − 146

16) 158 − 155

17) 135 − 134

18) 157 − 148

19) 159 − 142

20) 156 − 134

21) 158 − 155

22) 154 − 137

23) 160 − 131

24) 157 − 145

25) 141 − 136

26) 142 − 136

27) 156 − 156

28) 159 − 157

29) 156 − 148

30) 145 − 135

31) 146 − 137

32) 154 − 153

33) 155 − 147

34) 159 − 157

35) 153 − 132

36) 157 − 145

37) 157 − 153

38) 156 − 150

39) 153 − 134

40) 157 − 134

41) 135 − 135

42) 148 − 136

43) 142 − 135

44) 149 − 143

45) 149 − 140

46) 141 − 139

47) 148 − 138

48) 159 − 131

49) 142 − 139

50) 151 − 151

51) 158 − 148

52) 158 − 143

53) 134 − 134

54) 146 − 134

55) 147 − 132

56) 144 − 138

57) 160 − 157

58) 139 − 139

59) 133 − 133

60) 159 − 158

1) 158 − 142

2) 154 − 139

3) 149 − 145

4) 138 − 134

5) 150 − 140

6) 150 − 145

7) 155 − 133

8) 137 − 137

9) 157 − 144

10) 146 − 146

11) 138 − 138

12) 144 − 131

13) 135 − 133

14) 149 − 130

15) 155 − 155

16) 157 − 138

17) 157 − 134

18) 157 − 134

19) 155 − 134

20) 143 − 136

21) 149 − 141

22) 156 − 133

23) 147 − 135

24) 134 − 133

25) 144 − 132

26) 150 − 145

27) 130 − 130

28) 159 − 137

29) 144 − 142

30) 137 − 133

31) 156 − 145

32) 150 − 139

33) 148 − 142

34) 151 − 137

35) 153 − 140

36) 156 − 141

37) 145 − 142

38) 148 − 147

39) 160 − 160

40) 147 − 132

41) 154 − 137

42) 136 − 134

43) 142 − 131

44) 160 − 133

45) 151 − 151

46) 155 − 155

47) 147 − 141

48) 155 − 136

49) 159 − 132

50) 147 − 139

51) 151 − 134

52) 157 − 134

53) 157 − 146

54) 155 − 151

55) 157 − 145

56) 158 − 152

57) 142 − 135

58) 151 − 132

59) 151 − 136

60) 150 − 134

1) 160 − 137

2) 147 − 142

3) 155 − 146

4) 156 − 139

5) 155 − 155

6) 152 − 145

7) 136 − 132

8) 159 − 140

9) 134 − 133

10) 158 − 152

11) 155 − 154

12) 160 − 152

13) 145 − 145

14) 158 − 140

15) 147 − 133

16) 153 − 149

17) 153 − 135

18) 151 − 137

19) 160 − 158

20) 139 − 134

21) 148 − 143

22) 155 − 147

23) 137 − 137

24) 146 − 145

25) 142 − 140

26) 147 − 147

27) 154 − 138

28) 144 − 140

29) 149 − 135

30) 151 − 142

31) 154 − 133

32) 149 − 131

33) 159 − 133

34) 158 − 141

35) 148 − 147

36) 159 − 156

37) 159 − 152

38) 145 − 135

39) 148 − 139

40) 144 − 142

41) 143 − 135

42) 148 − 139

43) 160 − 152

44) 150 − 139

45) 156 − 147

46) 141 − 134

47) 157 − 131

48) 152 − 142

49) 149 − 134

50) 146 − 135

51) 139 − 135

52) 158 − 140

53) 153 − 137

54) 149 − 141

55) 141 − 130

56) 136 − 135

57) 145 − 137

58) 135 − 134

59) 158 − 148

60) 158 − 142

1) 149
    −[   ]
    19

2) [   ]
    − 132
    14

3) 145
    −[   ]
    6

4) [   ]
    − 135
    12

5) 152
    −[   ]
    6

6) [   ]
    − 139
    16

7) 159
    −[   ]
    5

8) [   ]
    − 131
    1

9) 137
    −[   ]
    5

10) [   ]
    − 130
    30

11) 157
    −[   ]
    23

12) [   ]
    − 139
    20

13) 153
    −[   ]
    5

14) [   ]
    − 132
    1

15) 148
    −[   ]
    7

16) [   ]
    − 135
    13

17) 149
    −[   ]
    3

18) [   ]
    − 141
    10

19) 159
    −[   ]
    1

20) [   ]
    − 131
    27

21) 140
    −[   ]
    7

22) [   ]
    − 139
    12

23) 145
    −[   ]
    3

24) [   ]
    − 130
    19

25) 138
    −[   ]
    5

26) [   ]
    − 131
    6

27) 137
    −[   ]
    7

28) [   ]
    − 137
    9

29) 143
    −[   ]
    9

30) [   ]
    − 146
    11

31) 149
    −[   ]
    7

32) [   ]
    − 131
    16

33) 157
    −[   ]
    9

34) [   ]
    − 134
    12

35) 152
    −[   ]
    22

36) [   ]
    − 131
    6

37) 154
    −[   ]
    19

38) [   ]
    − 135
    20

39) 160
    −[   ]
    10

40) [   ]
    − 142
    7

41) 157
    −[   ]
    20

42) [   ]
    − 143
    6

43) 143
    −[   ]
    12

44) [   ]
    − 157
    1

45) 151
    −[   ]
    20

46) [   ]
    − 132
    6

47) 130
    −[   ]
    0

48) [   ]
    − 144
    9

49) 142
    −[   ]
    6

50) [   ]
    − 144
    4

51) 160
    −[   ]
    4

52) [   ]
    − 148
    5

53) 158
    −[   ]
    18

54) [   ]
    − 135
    24

55) 140
    −[   ]
    4

56) [   ]
    − 156
    1

57) 158
    −[   ]
    3

58) [   ]
    − 155
    3

59) 150
    −[   ]
    11

60) [   ]
    − 134
    11

1) 144 − ☐ = 5

2) ☐ − 140 = 7

3) 159 − ☐ = 18

4) ☐ − 148 = 7

5) 146 − ☐ = 8

6) ☐ − 143 = 2

7) 156 − ☐ = 14

8) ☐ − 133 = 2

9) 134 − ☐ = 2

10) ☐ − 130 = 3

11) 157 − ☐ = 13

12) ☐ − 143 = 1

13) 151 − ☐ = 6

14) ☐ − 137 = 5

15) 160 − ☐ = 13

16) ☐ − 135 = 10

17) 146 − ☐ = 6

18) ☐ − 134 = 8

19) 141 − ☐ = 11

20) ☐ − 146 = 4

21) 157 − ☐ = 11

22) ☐ − 136 = 15

23) 159 − ☐ = 13

24) ☐ − 135 = 2

25) 150 − ☐ = 5

26) ☐ − 137 = 1

27) 153 − ☐ = 20

28) ☐ − 155 = 3

29) 159 − ☐ = 1

30) ☐ − 132 = 13

31) 156 − ☐ = 17

32) ☐ − 132 = 1

33) 158 − ☐ = 4

34) ☐ − 153 = 1

35) 143 − ☐ = 3

36) ☐ − 150 = 5

37) 150 − ☐ = 9

38) ☐ − 146 = 0

39) 140 − ☐ = 5

40) ☐ − 136 = 14

41) 153 − ☐ = 2

42) ☐ − 145 = 11

43) 156 − ☐ = 21

44) ☐ − 135 = 17

45) 143 − ☐ = 7

46) ☐ − 147 = 11

47) 160 − ☐ = 20

48) ☐ − 141 = 12

49) 157 − ☐ = 17

50) ☐ − 138 = 21

51) 133 − ☐ = 1

52) ☐ − 130 = 5

53) 158 − ☐ = 16

54) ☐ − 137 = 21

55) 160 − ☐ = 8

56) ☐ − 152 = 8

57) 142 − ☐ = 1

58) ☐ − 147 = 5

59) 152 − ☐ = 9

60) ☐ − 130 = 18

1)
$$138 - \boxed{} = 4$$

2)
$$\boxed{} - 143 = 4$$

3)
$$146 - \boxed{} = 16$$

4)
$$\boxed{} - 152 = 6$$

5)
$$141 - \boxed{} = 1$$

6)
$$\boxed{} - 142 = 10$$

7)
$$145 - \boxed{} = 11$$

8)
$$\boxed{} - 131 = 18$$

9)
$$138 - \boxed{} = 8$$

10)
$$\boxed{} - 140 = 18$$

11)
$$148 - \boxed{} = 14$$

12)
$$\boxed{} - 134 = 2$$

13)
$$131 - \boxed{} = 0$$

14)
$$\boxed{} - 150 = 4$$

15)
$$157 - \boxed{} = 19$$

16)
$$\boxed{} - 139 = 4$$

17)
$$153 - \boxed{} = 10$$

18)
$$\boxed{} - 141 = 16$$

19)
$$157 - \boxed{} = 26$$

20)
$$\boxed{} - 132 = 7$$

21)
$$146 - \boxed{} = 8$$

22)
$$\boxed{} - 132 = 12$$

23)
$$150 - \boxed{} = 17$$

24)
$$\boxed{} - 143 = 4$$

25)
$$149 - \boxed{} = 7$$

26)
$$\boxed{} - 136 = 10$$

27)
$$155 - \boxed{} = 1$$

28)
$$\boxed{} - 134 = 5$$

29)
$$148 - \boxed{} = 1$$

30)
$$\boxed{} - 149 = 11$$

31)
$$148 - \boxed{} = 4$$

32)
$$\boxed{} - 142 = 12$$

33)
$$158 - \boxed{} = 16$$

34)
$$\boxed{} - 137 = 9$$

35)
$$157 - \boxed{} = 9$$

36)
$$\boxed{} - 132 = 27$$

37)
$$152 - \boxed{} = 12$$

38)
$$\boxed{} - 134 = 17$$

39)
$$151 - \boxed{} = 13$$

40)
$$\boxed{} - 139 = 11$$

41)
$$146 - \boxed{} = 1$$

42)
$$\boxed{} - 132 = 22$$

43)
$$150 - \boxed{} = 1$$

44)
$$\boxed{} - 130 = 26$$

45)
$$138 - \boxed{} = 7$$

46)
$$\boxed{} - 130 = 24$$

47)
$$152 - \boxed{} = 14$$

48)
$$\boxed{} - 135 = 15$$

49)
$$158 - \boxed{} = 4$$

50)
$$\boxed{} - 152 = 8$$

51)
$$142 - \boxed{} = 10$$

52)
$$\boxed{} - 131 = 16$$

53)
$$154 - \boxed{} = 23$$

54)
$$\boxed{} - 141 = 11$$

55)
$$141 - \boxed{} = 5$$

56)
$$\boxed{} - 141 = 12$$

57)
$$160 - \boxed{} = 19$$

58)
$$\boxed{} - 150 = 4$$

59)
$$155 - \boxed{} = 5$$

60)
$$\boxed{} - 135 = 3$$

1) 134 − ☐ = 4

2) ☐ − 136 = 12

3) 144 − ☐ = 3

4) ☐ − 133 = 5

5) 150 − ☐ = 6

6) ☐ − 137 = 17

7) 154 − ☐ = 17

8) ☐ − 133 = 10

9) 141 − ☐ = 1

10) ☐ − 131 = 20

11) 144 − ☐ = 10

12) ☐ − 155 = 1

13) 153 − ☐ = 5

14) ☐ − 131 = 0

15) 158 − ☐ = 14

16) ☐ − 144 = 12

17) 148 − ☐ = 14

18) ☐ − 135 = 23

19) 160 − ☐ = 9

20) ☐ − 135 = 23

21) 148 − ☐ = 2

22) ☐ − 135 = 12

23) 147 − ☐ = 6

24) ☐ − 137 = 17

25) 149 − ☐ = 9

26) ☐ − 136 = 5

27) 160 − ☐ = 14

28) ☐ − 154 = 4

29) 149 − ☐ = 8

30) ☐ − 143 = 16

31) 149 − ☐ = 16

32) ☐ − 138 = 11

33) 146 − ☐ = 4

34) ☐ − 140 = 4

35) 157 − ☐ = 26

36) ☐ − 130 = 24

37) 159 − ☐ = 7

38) ☐ − 146 = 7

39) 157 − ☐ = 25

40) ☐ − 137 = 0

41) 133 − ☐ = 0

42) ☐ − 131 = 6

43) 144 − ☐ = 6

44) ☐ − 133 = 12

45) 154 − ☐ = 9

46) ☐ − 131 = 4

47) 149 − ☐ = 3

48) ☐ − 144 = 4

49) 159 − ☐ = 0

50) ☐ − 155 = 1

51) 154 − ☐ = 14

52) ☐ − 131 = 13

53) 159 − ☐ = 18

54) ☐ − 159 = 1

55) 159 − ☐ = 25

56) ☐ − 149 = 7

57) 152 − ☐ = 11

58) ☐ − 139 = 12

59) 156 − ☐ = 25

60) ☐ − 144 = 15

1) 149 − ☐ = 11

2) ☐ − 159 = 1

3) 135 − ☐ = 2

4) ☐ − 140 = 6

5) 151 − ☐ = 10

6) ☐ − 138 = 19

7) 148 − ☐ = 5

8) ☐ − 152 = 4

9) 156 − ☐ = 20

10) ☐ − 131 = 17

11) 158 − ☐ = 6

12) ☐ − 131 = 27

13) 157 − ☐ = 7

14) ☐ − 145 = 10

15) 160 − ☐ = 7

16) ☐ − 140 = 13

17) 140 − ☐ = 7

18) ☐ − 155 = 1

19) 158 − ☐ = 27

20) ☐ − 133 = 16

21) 151 − ☐ = 21

22) ☐ − 156 = 2

23) 147 − ☐ = 0

24) ☐ − 146 = 9

25) 142 − ☐ = 12

26) ☐ − 134 = 18

27) 156 − ☐ = 22

28) ☐ − 134 = 3

29) 147 − ☐ = 16

30) ☐ − 136 = 4

31) 144 − ☐ = 2

32) ☐ − 139 = 12

33) 148 − ☐ = 6

34) ☐ − 138 = 0

35) 148 − ☐ = 3

36) ☐ − 152 = 0

37) 160 − ☐ = 18

38) ☐ − 149 = 5

39) 150 − ☐ = 3

40) ☐ − 140 = 1

41) 145 − ☐ = 13

42) ☐ − 140 = 13

43) 142 − ☐ = 0

44) ☐ − 158 = 1

45) 152 − ☐ = 19

46) ☐ − 138 = 16

47) 156 − ☐ = 0

48) ☐ − 135 = 15

49) 152 − ☐ = 16

50) ☐ − 137 = 9

51) 158 − ☐ = 6

52) ☐ − 132 = 15

53) 140 − ☐ = 1

54) ☐ − 130 = 5

55) 154 − ☐ = 22

56) ☐ − 149 = 7

57) 149 − ☐ = 18

58) ☐ − 143 = 12

59) 150 − ☐ = 15

60) ☐ − 139 = 17

Page 1, Item 1:
(1)59 (2)62 (3)24 (4)34 (5)49 (6)43 (7)65
(8)45 (9)56 (10)59 (11)46 (12)38 (13)49
(14)34 (15)36 (16)43 (17)42 (18)43
(19)77 (20)45 (21)39 (22)47 (23)54
(24)47 (25)61 (26)41 (27)70 (28)47
(29)59 (30)49 (31)58 (32)43 (33)49
(34)30 (35)47 (36)35 (37)36 (38)37
(39)47 (40)32 (41)76 (42)33 (43)65
(44)48 (45)33 (46)52 (47)69 (48)69
(49)63 (50)42 (51)39 (52)58 (53)31
(54)64 (55)42 (56)49 (57)44 (58)56
(59)34 (60)47
Page 2, Item 1:
(1)75 (2)61 (3)53 (4)50 (5)43 (6)68 (7)40
(8)69 (9)45 (10)53 (11)44 (12)52 (13)58
(14)37 (15)53 (16)67 (17)39 (18)35
(19)30 (20)51 (21)51 (22)47 (23)48
(24)33 (25)74 (26)53 (27)71 (28)40
(29)50 (30)39 (31)49 (32)56 (33)59
(34)53 (35)75 (36)64 (37)51 (38)34
(39)48 (40)48 (41)57 (42)34 (43)36
(44)27 (45)44 (46)37 (47)38 (48)25
(49)47 (50)66 (51)44 (52)48 (53)31
(54)62 (55)61 (56)50 (57)58 (58)49
(59)54 (60)58
Page 3, Item 1:
(1)28 (2)55 (3)48 (4)49 (5)30 (6)38 (7)30
(8)62 (9)44 (10)50 (11)41 (12)43 (13)39
(14)56 (15)73 (16)51 (17)58 (18)39
(19)47 (20)37 (21)66 (22)53 (23)35
(24)49 (25)52 (26)42 (27)50 (28)64
(29)50 (30)58 (31)50 (32)63 (33)76
(34)45 (35)50 (36)37 (37)80 (38)30
(39)61 (40)47 (41)56 (42)53 (43)36
(44)43 (45)36 (46)51 (47)33 (48)54

(49)43 (50)36 (51)61 (52)31 (53)28
(54)43 (55)57 (56)48 (57)50 (58)57
(59)56 (60)29
Page 4, Item 1:
(1)50 (2)71 (3)43 (4)48 (5)77 (6)36 (7)49
(8)68 (9)42 (10)57 (11)30 (12)70 (13)65
(14)62 (15)51 (16)34 (17)39 (18)48
(19)40 (20)51 (21)61 (22)35 (23)51
(24)32 (25)44 (26)67 (27)41 (28)48
(29)48 (30)60 (31)76 (32)57 (33)58
(34)67 (35)65 (36)55 (37)61 (38)44
(39)44 (40)59 (41)34 (42)29 (43)48
(44)68 (45)54 (46)34 (47)61 (48)26
(49)55 (50)46 (51)40 (52)55 (53)41
(54)50 (55)69 (56)72 (57)71 (58)39
(59)42 (60)31
Page 5, Item 1:
(1)63 (2)64 (3)68 (4)76 (5)43 (6)49 (7)60
(8)21 (9)46 (10)49 (11)52 (12)37 (13)44
(14)48 (15)54 (16)45 (17)34 (18)27
(19)67 (20)30 (21)26 (22)25 (23)42
(24)26 (25)50 (26)61 (27)40 (28)50
(29)52 (30)56 (31)45 (32)55 (33)47
(34)72 (35)48 (36)77 (37)55 (38)70
(39)57 (40)61 (41)41 (42)39 (43)39
(44)62 (45)35 (46)23 (47)45 (48)64
(49)50 (50)55 (51)51 (52)40 (53)23
(54)61 (55)44 (56)71 (57)33 (58)35
(59)40 (60)66
Page 6, Item 1:
(1)12 (2)32 (3)40 (4)17 (5)25 (6)31 (7)26
(8)17 (9)40 (10)37 (11)36 (12)11 (13)23
(14)29 (15)24 (16)16 (17)16 (18)37
(19)11 (20)17 (21)17 (22)20 (23)26
(24)22 (25)31 (26)37 (27)27 (28)40
(29)20 (30)22 (31)37 (32)37 (33)32

(38)14 (39)20 (40)26 (41)13 (42)10
(43)13 (44)18 (45)12 (46)33 (47)13
(48)21 (49)32 (50)11 (51)36 (52)24
(53)14 (54)35 (55)39 (56)18 (57)21
(58)25 (59)20 (60)20

Page 7, Item 1:
(1)29 (2)37 (3)12 (4)36 (5)34 (6)23 (7)35
(8)23 (9)28 (10)32 (11)32 (12)23 (13)25
(14)18 (15)37 (16)39 (17)37 (18)28
(19)17 (20)34 (21)27 (22)30 (23)13
(24)24 (25)12 (26)21 (27)12 (28)31
(29)12 (30)27 (31)30 (32)10 (33)39
(34)30 (35)35 (36)40 (37)14 (38)38
(39)21 (40)18 (41)10 (42)24 (43)39
(44)28 (45)29 (46)22 (47)18 (48)29
(49)22 (50)18 (51)18 (52)38 (53)11
(54)19 (55)20 (56)22 (57)21 (58)18
(59)28 (60)13

Page 8, Item 1:
(1)18 (2)33 (3)18 (4)18 (5)20 (6)35 (7)22
(8)30 (9)38 (10)10 (11)13 (12)34 (13)32
(14)28 (15)20 (16)12 (17)29 (18)30
(19)14 (20)29 (21)30 (22)34 (23)11
(24)32 (25)35 (26)12 (27)23 (28)12
(29)31 (30)22 (31)31 (32)19 (33)17
(34)32 (35)38 (36)28 (37)12 (38)32
(39)30 (40)22 (41)11 (42)33 (43)20
(44)28 (45)34 (46)30 (47)32 (48)38
(49)13 (50)40 (51)22 (52)26 (53)34
(54)31 (55)38 (56)25 (57)11 (58)10
(59)15 (60)10

Page 9, Item 1:
(1)39 (2)40 (3)19 (4)16 (5)32 (6)22 (7)15
(8)22 (9)12 (10)11 (11)37 (12)18 (13)40
(14)27 (15)37 (16)20 (17)16 (18)30
(19)29 (20)37 (21)40 (22)24 (23)24

(24)13 (25)24 (26)10 (27)39 (28)22
(29)36 (30)27 (31)11 (32)10 (33)18
(34)35 (35)23 (36)22 (37)16 (38)13
(39)15 (40)12 (41)38 (42)20 (43)31
(44)26 (45)23 (46)23 (47)38 (48)24
(49)12 (50)10 (51)27 (52)31 (53)40
(54)30 (55)27 (56)28 (57)30 (58)29
(59)39 (60)34

Page 10, Item 1:
(1)27 (2)33 (3)40 (4)40 (5)19 (6)40 (7)24
(8)19 (9)15 (10)34 (11)28 (12)11 (13)30
(14)19 (15)11 (16)15 (17)32 (18)16
(19)33 (20)17 (21)21 (22)23 (23)12
(24)12 (25)22 (26)20 (27)17 (28)40
(29)10 (30)21 (31)30 (32)31 (33)40
(34)13 (35)33 (36)11 (37)20 (38)29
(39)23 (40)36 (41)22 (42)15 (43)17
(44)40 (45)28 (46)30 (47)15 (48)20
(49)36 (50)39 (51)37 (52)25 (53)11
(54)39 (55)39 (56)16 (57)11 (58)14
(59)30 (60)31

Page 11, Item 1:
(1)107 (2)86 (3)128 (4)128 (5)117 (6)109
(7)124 (8)124 (9)86 (10)136 (11)106
(12)127 (13)133 (14)123 (15)115 (16)103
(17)122 (18)121 (19)118 (20)105 (21)109
(22)113 (23)108 (24)125 (25)100 (26)102
(27)136 (28)113 (29)138 (30)107 (31)110
(32)113 (33)135 (34)127 (35)97 (36)95
(37)84 (38)106 (39)106 (40)106 (41)91
(42)115 (43)109 (44)139 (45)101 (46)114
(47)113 (48)116 (49)118 (50)91 (51)116
(52)104 (53)136 (54)96 (55)130 (56)97
(57)90 (58)109 (59)86 (60)119

Page 12, Item 1:
(1)106 (2)88 (3)124 (4)115 (5)116 (6)129

(12)111 (13)124 (14)114 (15)98 (16)119
(17)85 (18)110 (19)100 (20)114 (21)122
(22)118 (23)103 (24)121 (25)106 (26)112
(27)107 (28)137 (29)96 (30)81 (31)111
(32)96 (33)107 (34)124 (35)97 (36)120
(37)85 (38)104 (39)135 (40)135 (41)116
(42)113 (43)103 (44)90 (45)129 (46)121
(47)100 (48)123 (49)95 (50)97 (51)113
(52)132 (53)100 (54)127 (55)96 (56)137
(57)85 (58)137 (59)113 (60)135

Page 13, Item 1:
(1)102 (2)111 (3)130 (4)112 (5)128 (6)89
(7)111 (8)115 (9)113 (10)113 (11)101
(12)123 (13)95 (14)103 (15)125 (16)108
(17)108 (18)104 (19)110 (20)123 (21)119
(22)99 (23)93 (24)124 (25)106 (26)103
(27)118 (28)105 (29)110 (30)118 (31)118
(32)107 (33)88 (34)110 (35)105 (36)136
(37)102 (38)103 (39)125 (40)117 (41)120
(42)130 (43)92 (44)124 (45)108 (46)121
(47)122 (48)103 (49)115 (50)115 (51)114
(52)124 (53)90 (54)97 (55)135 (56)128
(57)124 (58)102 (59)104 (60)124

Page 14, Item 1:
(1)91 (2)90 (3)127 (4)113 (5)100 (6)97
(7)89 (8)131 (9)109 (10)129 (11)93
(12)96 (13)109 (14)108 (15)101 (16)102
(17)104 (18)95 (19)111 (20)110 (21)102
(22)109 (23)109 (24)106 (25)116 (26)97
(27)129 (28)111 (29)93 (30)107 (31)119
(32)99 (33)106 (34)131 (35)110 (36)112
(37)95 (38)104 (39)138 (40)102 (41)121
(42)97 (43)100 (44)103 (45)113 (46)125
(47)110 (48)105 (49)104 (50)114 (51)129
(52)119 (53)124 (54)101 (55)114 (56)97
(57)98 (58)98 (59)100 (60)123

Page 15, Item 1:
(1)116 (2)124 (3)108 (4)123 (5)110
(6)102 (7)117 (8)104 (9)108 (10)128
(11)123 (12)97 (13)104 (14)116 (15)115
(16)110 (17)129 (18)103 (19)131 (20)125
(21)114 (22)98 (23)85 (24)125 (25)100
(26)85 (27)128 (28)107 (29)119 (30)101
(31)97 (32)97 (33)91 (34)89 (35)101
(36)118 (37)84 (38)122 (39)123 (40)111
(41)123 (42)101 (43)106 (44)104 (45)115
(46)86 (47)122 (48)99 (49)105 (50)129
(51)93 (52)117 (53)81 (54)113 (55)111
(56)121 (57)97 (58)101 (59)119 (60)109

Page 16, Item 1:
(1)54 (2)42 (3)44 (4)66 (5)62 (6)62 (7)63
(8)55 (9)68 (10)66 (11)63 (12)65 (13)44
(14)57 (15)44 (16)59 (17)46 (18)68
(19)49 (20)42 (21)47 (22)60 (23)54
(24)69 (25)67 (26)63 (27)46 (28)57
(29)61 (30)64 (31)59 (32)64 (33)46
(34)69 (35)60 (36)41 (37)48 (38)51
(39)68 (40)62 (41)61 (42)56 (43)41
(44)63 (45)49 (46)44 (47)53 (48)70
(49)43 (50)60 (51)61 (52)45 (53)66
(54)44 (55)42 (56)53 (57)50 (58)45
(59)63 (60)49

Page 17, Item 1:
(1)45 (2)50 (3)45 (4)46 (5)56 (6)40 (7)67
(8)66 (9)56 (10)57 (11)48 (12)62 (13)56

(14)67 (15)59 (16)53 (17)50 (18)47
(19)52 (20)70 (21)45 (22)67 (23)59
(24)60 (25)67 (26)59 (27)48 (28)54
(29)62 (30)54 (31)47 (32)63 (33)46
(34)51 (35)62 (36)61 (37)46 (38)49
(39)42 (40)44 (41)63 (42)53 (43)47
(44)60 (45)50 (46)42 (47)69 (48)61
(49)63 (50)44 (51)46 (52)47 (53)46
(54)41 (55)45 (56)44 (57)45 (58)64
(59)69 (60)53

Page 18, Item 1:

(1)42 (2)63 (3)52 (4)54 (5)44 (6)40 (7)44
(8)57 (9)43 (10)53 (11)52 (12)49 (13)44
(14)67 (15)61 (16)58 (17)64 (18)61
(19)63 (20)60 (21)40 (22)69 (23)69
(24)48 (25)41 (26)61 (27)53 (28)44
(29)70 (30)51 (31)45 (32)43 (33)52
(34)63 (35)59 (36)48 (37)46 (38)53
(39)52 (40)53 (41)65 (42)53 (43)46
(44)42 (45)44 (46)50 (47)48 (48)40
(49)67 (50)41 (51)56 (52)53 (53)41
(54)43 (55)45 (56)40 (57)68 (58)53
(59)45 (60)52

Page 19, Item 1:

(1)46 (2)68 (3)64 (4)47 (5)47 (6)55 (7)61
(8)60 (9)42 (10)70 (11)40 (12)62 (13)40
(14)47 (15)46 (16)47 (17)53 (18)62
(19)66 (20)43 (21)52 (22)45 (23)69
(24)49 (25)61 (26)48 (27)64 (28)55
(29)61 (30)44 (31)47 (32)48 (33)57
(34)41 (35)41 (36)54 (37)54 (38)51
(39)57 (40)62 (41)66 (42)57 (43)60
(44)61 (45)52 (46)61 (47)66 (48)67
(49)55 (50)60 (51)68 (52)50 (53)67
(54)64 (55)69 (56)66 (57)67 (58)45
(59)50 (60)70

Page 20, Item 1:

(1)44 (2)44 (3)51 (4)57 (5)67 (6)44 (7)42
(8)44 (9)46 (10)42 (11)64 (12)54 (13)56
(14)51 (15)62 (16)53 (17)47 (18)44
(19)45 (20)52 (21)50 (22)55 (23)50
(24)49 (25)48 (26)70 (27)69 (28)54
(29)48 (30)65 (31)42 (32)63 (33)55
(34)63 (35)50 (36)57 (37)44 (38)55
(39)54 (40)55 (41)53 (42)65 (43)42
(44)41 (45)55 (46)42 (47)64 (48)63
(49)58 (50)59 (51)54 (52)63 (53)58
(54)53 (55)57 (56)52 (57)58 (58)58
(59)65 (60)63

Page 21, Item 1:

(1)175 (2)182 (3)175 (4)187 (5)166
(6)184 (7)145 (8)168 (9)161 (10)155
(11)144 (12)180 (13)173 (14)153 (15)156
(16)172 (17)173 (18)185 (19)183 (20)174
(21)164 (22)172 (23)192 (24)194 (25)184
(26)148 (27)168 (28)185 (29)158 (30)161
(31)165 (32)154 (33)176 (34)160 (35)193
(36)152 (37)147 (38)171 (39)148 (40)151
(41)175 (42)176 (43)151 (44)168 (45)169
(46)155 (47)169 (48)188 (49)171 (50)173
(51)161 (52)175 (53)175 (54)160 (55)178
(56)165 (57)166 (58)168 (59)174 (60)161

Page 22, Item 1:

(1)159 (2)168 (3)147 (4)144 (5)142
(6)153 (7)161 (8)157 (9)162 (10)146
(11)143 (12)158 (13)144 (14)140 (15)169
(16)164 (17)150 (18)165 (19)144 (20)154
(21)164 (22)163 (23)169 (24)154 (25)163
(26)164 (27)143 (28)160 (29)168 (30)162
(31)143 (32)148 (33)142 (34)156 (35)166
(36)168

(37)159 (38)158 (39)143 (40)149 (41)152
(42)142 (43)146 (44)164 (45)161 (46)170
(47)166 (48)169 (49)153 (50)168 (51)144
(52)149 (53)168 (54)140 (55)166 (56)162
(57)168 (58)160 (59)170 (60)165
Page 23, Item 1:
(1)182 (2)179 (3)159 (4)169 (5)185
(6)177 (7)153 (8)170 (9)168 (10)172
(11)172 (12)163 (13)170 (14)166 (15)177
(16)162 (17)171 (18)165 (19)158 (20)148
(21)195 (22)169 (23)155 (24)169 (25)165
(26)169 (27)155 (28)153 (29)169 (30)156
(31)163 (32)158 (33)171 (34)170 (35)144
(36)151 (37)182 (38)166 (39)175 (40)159
(41)191 (42)183 (43)152 (44)153 (45)186
(46)200 (47)158 (48)159 (49)188 (50)162
(51)148 (52)166 (53)155 (54)155 (55)157
(56)170 (57)194 (58)156 (59)140 (60)171
Page 24, Item 1:
(1)193 (2)169 (3)147 (4)169 (5)179
(6)162 (7)158 (8)186 (9)185 (10)172
(11)193 (12)176 (13)161 (14)178 (15)162
(16)161 (17)176 (18)149 (19)191 (20)140
(21)189 (22)174 (23)150 (24)168 (25)164
(26)158 (27)180 (28)182 (29)173 (30)177
(31)171 (32)178 (33)162 (34)185 (35)167
(36)163 (37)174 (38)179 (39)168 (40)183
(41)180 (42)148 (43)160 (44)178 (45)149
(46)173 (47)157 (48)155 (49)164 (50)185
(51)178 (52)162 (53)167 (54)182 (55)147
(56)155 (57)180 (58)184 (59)155 (60)188
Page 25, Item 1:
(1)186 (2)179 (3)174 (4)170 (5)169
(6)187 (7)177 (8)186 (9)164 (10)150
(11)162 (12)165 (13)176 (14)169 (15)156
(16)168 (17)173 (18)154 (19)171 (20)172

(21)165 (22)181 (23)162 (24)162 (25)167
(26)172 (27)172 (28)200 (29)149 (30)166
(31)160 (32)152 (33)163 (34)170 (35)163
(36)171 (37)156 (38)167 (39)160 (40)193
(41)182 (42)190 (43)166 (44)184 (45)170
(46)167 (47)190 (48)159 (49)168 (50)164
(51)187 (52)184 (53)174 (54)159 (55)183
(56)171 (57)157 (58)155 (59)174 (60)184
Page 26, Item 1:
(1)80 (2)100 (3)93 (4)73 (5)74 (6)86 (7)95
(8)84 (9)93 (10)86 (11)82 (12)84 (13)99
(14)81 (15)83 (16)90 (17)98 (18)79
(19)93 (20)93 (21)85 (22)95 (23)76
(24)100 (25)80 (26)76 (27)86 (28)86
(29)86 (30)71 (31)87 (32)93 (33)85
(34)85 (35)71 (36)78 (37)71 (38)89
(39)71 (40)83 (41)100 (42)76 (43)95
(44)83 (45)94 (46)76 (47)92 (48)85
(49)80 (50)74 (51)81 (52)80 (53)75
(54)94 (55)74 (56)96 (57)85 (58)83
(59)71 (60)100
Page 27, Item 1:
(1)72 (2)73 (3)79 (4)81 (5)94 (6)79 (7)76
(8)74 (9)80 (10)75 (11)95 (12)73 (13)90
(14)88 (15)81 (16)73 (17)96 (18)75
(19)70 (20)83 (21)70 (22)82 (23)100
(24)72 (25)73 (26)79 (27)100 (28)100
(29)78 (30)90 (31)89 (32)73 (33)93
(34)99 (35)82

(36)92 (37)99 (38)71 (39)75 (40)90
(41)98 (42)71 (43)100 (44)98 (45)97
(46)79 (47)85 (48)82 (49)97 (50)96
(51)85 (52)71 (53)94 (54)99 (55)91
(56)92 (57)87 (58)97 (59)86 (60)75

Page 28, Item 1:
(1)78 (2)97 (3)82 (4)90 (5)99 (6)94 (7)94
(8)71 (9)74 (10)74 (11)98 (12)72 (13)93
(14)78 (15)89 (16)90 (17)99 (18)100
(19)76 (20)73 (21)73 (22)91 (23)83
(24)71 (25)77 (26)72 (27)100 (28)74
(29)76 (30)99 (31)82 (32)91 (33)85
(34)84 (35)89 (36)71 (37)86 (38)90
(39)97 (40)96 (41)88 (42)91 (43)70
(44)84 (45)78 (46)75 (47)74 (48)73
(49)88 (50)96 (51)77 (52)98 (53)97
(54)96 (55)95 (56)80 (57)96 (58)92
(59)88 (60)74

Page 29, Item 1:
(1)88 (2)74 (3)92 (4)92 (5)92 (6)75 (7)71
(8)90 (9)91 (10)96 (11)80 (12)98 (13)77
(14)94 (15)96 (16)92 (17)89 (18)82
(19)84 (20)79 (21)99 (22)94 (23)76
(24)82 (25)95 (26)88 (27)78 (28)79
(29)74 (30)84 (31)96 (32)100 (33)81
(34)72 (35)72 (36)84 (37)93 (38)74
(39)100 (40)70 (41)95 (42)74 (43)77
(44)97 (45)70 (46)78 (47)100 (48)78
(49)71 (50)82 (51)83 (52)91 (53)95
(54)89 (55)82 (56)79 (57)71 (58)88
(59)99 (60)89

Page 30, Item 1:
(1)92 (2)77 (3)85 (4)78 (5)81 (6)87 (7)76
(8)98 (9)71 (10)99 (11)71 (12)80 (13)78
(14)82 (15)90 (16)82 (17)80 (18)77
(19)85 (20)85 (21)84 (22)92 (23)89

(24)82 (25)71 (26)95 (27)84 (28)88
(29)74 (30)75 (31)94 (32)93 (33)87
(34)100 (35)73 (36)94 (37)97 (38)76
(39)74 (40)72 (41)90 (42)89 (43)74
(44)71 (45)73 (46)88 (47)81 (48)78
(49)76 (50)80 (51)93 (52)92 (53)99
(54)95 (55)78 (56)81 (57)84 (58)74
(59)78 (60)89

Page 31, Item 1:
(1)225 (2)235 (3)215 (4)235 (5)236
(6)224 (7)232 (8)218 (9)215 (10)216
(11)219 (12)224 (13)220 (14)225 (15)224
(16)237 (17)251 (18)223 (19)245 (20)233
(21)238 (22)226 (23)214 (24)219 (25)214
(26)245 (27)239 (28)238 (29)209 (30)243
(31)230 (32)220 (33)243 (34)249 (35)243
(36)251 (37)238 (38)204 (39)210 (40)249
(41)215 (42)227 (43)238 (44)248 (45)235
(46)224 (47)246 (48)228 (49)211 (50)232
(51)241 (52)233 (53)218 (54)230 (55)251
(56)260 (57)204 (58)232 (59)223 (60)238

Page 32, Item 1:
(1)236 (2)222 (3)213 (4)237 (5)225
(6)232 (7)224 (8)213 (9)240 (10)218
(11)257 (12)237 (13)227 (14)237 (15)220
(16)230 (17)213 (18)236 (19)239 (20)224
(21)202 (22)223 (23)229 (24)230 (25)224
(26)223 (27)242 (28)248 (29)234 (30)237
(31)232 (32)217 (33)223 (34)218 (35)224
(36)231 (37)243 (38)234 (39)251 (40)235
(41)252 (42)230 (43)233 (44)246 (45)211
(46)239

(47)249 (48)249 (49)237 (50)248 (51)226
(52)226 (53)236 (54)220 (55)211 (56)237
(57)234 (58)228 (59)242 (60)232
Page 33, Item 1:
(1)244 (2)238 (3)229 (4)224 (5)245
(6)206 (7)247 (8)244 (9)227 (10)227
(11)242 (12)224 (13)226 (14)226 (15)235
(16)239 (17)209 (18)218 (19)255 (20)220
(21)234 (22)219 (23)207 (24)238 (25)232
(26)213 (27)249 (28)254 (29)227 (30)237
(31)247 (32)203 (33)248 (34)254 (35)221
(36)238 (37)238 (38)229 (39)213 (40)229
(41)225 (42)225 (43)229 (44)227 (45)231
(46)221 (47)235 (48)226 (49)219 (50)227
(51)246 (52)242 (53)204 (54)237 (55)215
(56)258 (57)222 (58)243 (59)229 (60)215
Page 34, Item 1:
(1)212 (2)212 (3)229 (4)244 (5)223
(6)227 (7)214 (8)216 (9)226 (10)220
(11)207 (12)239 (13)234 (14)210 (15)230
(16)229 (17)248 (18)221 (19)218 (20)221
(21)216 (22)225 (23)212 (24)228 (25)243
(26)230 (27)238 (28)237 (29)240 (30)228
(31)231 (32)228 (33)236 (34)253 (35)234
(36)225 (37)234 (38)228 (39)244 (40)229
(41)251 (42)230 (43)227 (44)223 (45)233
(46)239 (47)205 (48)242 (49)218 (50)242
(51)233 (52)248 (53)222 (54)233 (55)234
(56)224 (57)226 (58)230 (59)235 (60)233
Page 35, Item 1:
(1)229 (2)209 (3)216 (4)224 (5)237
(6)230 (7)247 (8)243 (9)207 (10)249
(11)231 (12)227 (13)230 (14)243 (15)240
(16)230 (17)248 (18)218 (19)219 (20)220
(21)236 (22)239 (23)234 (24)207 (25)239
(26)241 (27)224 (28)231 (29)231 (30)231

(31)212 (32)242 (33)222 (34)252 (35)251
(36)241 (37)236 (38)220 (39)227 (40)220
(41)239 (42)221 (43)240 (44)232 (45)254
(46)221 (47)233 (48)205 (49)227 (50)217
(51)246 (52)251 (53)224 (54)212 (55)243
(56)234 (57)242 (58)246 (59)205 (60)201
Page 36, Item 1:
(1)113 (2)105 (3)106 (4)105 (5)108
(6)100 (7)107 (8)103 (9)101 (10)106
(11)117 (12)111 (13)127 (14)130 (15)119
(16)114 (17)123 (18)106 (19)105 (20)115
(21)130 (22)114 (23)108 (24)103 (25)123
(26)109 (27)115 (28)126 (29)118 (30)106
(31)115 (32)127 (33)110 (34)112 (35)120
(36)106 (37)108 (38)123 (39)115 (40)126
(41)112 (42)103 (43)126 (44)103 (45)121
(46)111 (47)119 (48)108 (49)120 (50)130
(51)111 (52)109 (53)112 (54)117 (55)100
(56)111 (57)107 (58)112 (59)115 (60)105
Page 37, Item 1:
(1)121 (2)112 (3)107 (4)107 (5)111
(6)126 (7)126 (8)127 (9)100 (10)103
(11)114 (12)120 (13)104 (14)116 (15)122
(16)108 (17)112 (18)128 (19)130 (20)111
(21)107 (22)103 (23)127 (24)127 (25)130
(26)117 (27)105 (28)128 (29)109 (30)118
(31)102 (32)107 (33)118 (34)111 (35)130
(36)104

(37)119 (38)113 (39)105 (40)109 (41)123
(42)120 (43)126 (44)122 (45)109 (46)120
(47)103 (48)100 (49)124 (50)100 (51)114
(52)120 (53)119 (54)123 (55)127 (56)105
(57)103 (58)101 (59)112 (60)128

Page 38, Item 1:

(1)115 (2)115 (3)100 (4)100 (5)100
(6)120 (7)128 (8)127 (9)104 (10)115
(11)103 (12)126 (13)125 (14)114 (15)113
(16)129 (17)114 (18)125 (19)116 (20)102
(21)118 (22)130 (23)121 (24)121 (25)126
(26)116 (27)108 (28)127 (29)107 (30)101
(31)124 (32)102 (33)117 (34)102 (35)108
(36)101 (37)116 (38)113 (39)103 (40)129
(41)100 (42)115 (43)122 (44)105 (45)116
(46)121 (47)124 (48)113 (49)101 (50)118
(51)121 (52)115 (53)109 (54)112 (55)106
(56)102 (57)123 (58)122 (59)127 (60)117

Page 39, Item 1:

(1)116 (2)121 (3)121 (4)111 (5)124
(6)101 (7)114 (8)102 (9)115 (10)127
(11)113 (12)121 (13)122 (14)128 (15)102
(16)105 (17)116 (18)118 (19)119 (20)109
(21)101 (22)121 (23)118 (24)105 (25)108
(26)101 (27)123 (28)113 (29)110 (30)117
(31)120 (32)114 (33)116 (34)100 (35)122
(36)123 (37)128 (38)117 (39)123 (40)123
(41)119 (42)111 (43)110 (44)105 (45)103
(46)108 (47)129 (48)116 (49)130 (50)114
(51)113 (52)105 (53)124 (54)119 (55)107
(56)101 (57)102 (58)128 (59)123 (60)102

Page 40, Item 1:

(1)110 (2)109 (3)113 (4)100 (5)119
(6)124 (7)130 (8)100 (9)117 (10)105
(11)102 (12)113 (13)123 (14)128 (15)104
(16)115 (17)117 (18)108 (19)126 (20)105

(21)108 (22)119 (23)107 (24)112 (25)104
(26)108 (27)105 (28)116 (29)108 (30)127
(31)117 (32)125 (33)115 (34)102 (35)124
(36)108 (37)125 (38)107 (39)122 (40)113
(41)128 (42)113 (43)107 (44)115 (45)124
(46)124 (47)122 (48)105 (49)112 (50)125
(51)112 (52)113 (53)119 (54)102 (55)102
(56)124 (57)117 (58)107 (59)109 (60)129

Page 41, Item 1:

(1)310 (2)294 (3)283 (4)311 (5)273
(6)285 (7)273 (8)264 (9)315 (10)295
(11)293 (12)307 (13)298 (14)277 (15)268
(16)280 (17)294 (18)267 (19)305 (20)276
(21)290 (22)291 (23)303 (24)268 (25)308
(26)298 (27)303 (28)288 (29)292 (30)289
(31)303 (32)297 (33)280 (34)266 (35)291
(36)314 (37)278 (38)315 (39)297 (40)294
(41)282 (42)270 (43)312 (44)294 (45)290
(46)284 (47)315 (48)279 (49)300 (50)303
(51)283 (52)295 (53)304 (54)288 (55)289
(56)265 (57)296 (58)279 (59)280 (60)282

Page 42, Item 1:

(1)281 (2)265 (3)295 (4)292 (5)288
(6)291 (7)289 (8)304 (9)268 (10)276
(11)302 (12)285 (13)307 (14)308 (15)293
(16)284 (17)279 (18)300 (19)292 (20)288
(21)272 (22)270 (23)282 (24)283 (25)295
(26)307

(27)291 (28)308 (29)298 (30)279 (31)293
(32)301 (33)281 (34)291 (35)316 (36)272
(37)269 (38)283 (39)280 (40)287 (41)285
(42)299 (43)302 (44)291 (45)317 (46)301
(47)270 (48)281 (49)284 (50)301 (51)278
(52)283 (53)306 (54)278 (55)266 (56)308
(57)282 (58)280 (59)295 (60)297
Page 43, Item 1:
(1)290 (2)267 (3)307 (4)278 (5)298
(6)265 (7)299 (8)285 (9)307 (10)316
(11)283 (12)305 (13)304 (14)285 (15)303
(16)275 (17)293 (18)291 (19)281 (20)285
(21)287 (22)300 (23)285 (24)285 (25)269
(26)304 (27)288 (28)301 (29)312 (30)303
(31)297 (32)301 (33)260 (34)302 (35)294
(36)278 (37)294 (38)290 (39)300 (40)274
(41)284 (42)287 (43)286 (44)297 (45)294
(46)283 (47)301 (48)305 (49)301 (50)309
(51)284 (52)293 (53)310 (54)293 (55)308
(56)300 (57)314 (58)289 (59)302 (60)294
Page 44, Item 1:
(1)288 (2)301 (3)264 (4)302 (5)291
(6)300 (7)275 (8)274 (9)277 (10)285
(11)279 (12)300 (13)288 (14)295 (15)301
(16)300 (17)318 (18)280 (19)299 (20)276
(21)277 (22)302 (23)285 (24)297 (25)276
(26)291 (27)279 (28)293 (29)298 (30)291
(31)308 (32)302 (33)301 (34)283 (35)282
(36)270 (37)305 (38)290 (39)276 (40)295
(41)277 (42)301 (43)279 (44)276 (45)277
(46)298 (47)290 (48)292 (49)271 (50)311
(51)289 (52)280 (53)274 (54)278 (55)307
(56)278 (57)293 (58)296 (59)283 (60)284
Page 45, Item 1:
(1)286 (2)283 (3)304 (4)295 (5)286
(6)287 (7)273 (8)288 (9)286 (10)299

(11)281 (12)285 (13)286 (14)263 (15)288
(16)280 (17)280 (18)280 (19)299 (20)269
(21)312 (22)293 (23)285 (24)283 (25)289
(26)314 (27)294 (28)289 (29)296 (30)281
(31)294 (32)298 (33)293 (34)288 (35)293
(36)296 (37)267 (38)283 (39)303 (40)286
(41)306 (42)290 (43)280 (44)304 (45)277
(46)315 (47)292 (48)292 (49)306 (50)284
(51)296 (52)283 (53)279 (54)265 (55)279
(56)273 (57)300 (58)266 (59)316 (60)309
Page 46, Item 1:
(1)147 (2)135 (3)142 (4)158 (5)141
(6)137 (7)151 (8)149 (9)157 (10)140
(11)155 (12)146 (13)140 (14)130 (15)149
(16)144 (17)154 (18)150 (19)153 (20)157
(21)159 (22)149 (23)152 (24)138 (25)132
(26)141 (27)156 (28)141 (29)140 (30)141
(31)131 (32)130 (33)144 (34)160 (35)149
(36)150 (37)135 (38)147 (39)134 (40)135
(41)146 (42)141 (43)160 (44)134 (45)134
(46)139 (47)151 (48)146 (49)160 (50)136
(51)146 (52)143 (53)158 (54)149 (55)142
(56)144 (57)140 (58)150 (59)132 (60)159
Page 47, Item 1:
(1)159 (2)146 (3)149 (4)152 (5)153
(6)155 (7)138 (8)130 (9)132 (10)160
(11)137

(12)131 (13)130 (14)155 (15)144 (16)142
(17)152 (18)152 (19)138 (20)133 (21)150
(22)149 (23)140 (24)144 (25)135 (26)153
(27)140 (28)131 (29)143 (30)154 (31)136
(32)132 (33)143 (34)132 (35)145 (36)135
(37)133 (38)145 (39)147 (40)155 (41)136
(42)142 (43)148 (44)140 (45)152 (46)158
(47)147 (48)146 (49)154 (50)154 (51)157
(52)144 (53)149 (54)146 (55)136 (56)132
(57)156 (58)153 (59)155 (60)143

Page 48, Item 1:

(1)146 (2)141 (3)150 (4)144 (5)141
(6)160 (7)142 (8)144 (9)143 (10)144
(11)153 (12)142 (13)149 (14)145 (15)133
(16)143 (17)160 (18)145 (19)151 (20)157
(21)152 (22)143 (23)148 (24)150 (25)151
(26)158 (27)139 (28)154 (29)132 (30)149
(31)141 (32)153 (33)131 (34)143 (35)159
(36)137 (37)150 (38)146 (39)159 (40)140
(41)136 (42)149 (43)136 (44)138 (45)152
(46)142 (47)156 (48)152 (49)160 (50)152
(51)135 (52)152 (53)158 (54)156 (55)153
(56)138 (57)155 (58)135 (59)152 (60)135

Page 49, Item 1:

(1)137 (2)152 (3)147 (4)156 (5)134
(6)134 (7)141 (8)140 (9)141 (10)144
(11)152 (12)138 (13)145 (14)140 (15)148
(16)137 (17)143 (18)138 (19)147 (20)153
(21)141 (22)139 (23)153 (24)137 (25)130
(26)152 (27)136 (28)149 (29)144 (30)149
(31)149 (32)145 (33)152 (34)145 (35)134
(36)149 (37)143 (38)131 (39)160 (40)157
(41)159 (42)134 (43)155 (44)141 (45)138
(46)130 (47)150 (48)152 (49)137 (50)150
(51)149 (52)151 (53)156 (54)157 (55)154
(56)159 (57)143 (58)133 (59)132 (60)142

Page 50, Item 1:

(1)141 (2)139 (3)152 (4)133 (5)134
(6)148 (7)145 (8)147 (9)153 (10)151
(11)131 (12)154 (13)135 (14)130 (15)132
(16)138 (17)145 (18)139 (19)154 (20)144
(21)150 (22)148 (23)136 (24)154 (25)138
(26)143 (27)144 (28)159 (29)131 (30)130
(31)159 (32)149 (33)159 (34)130 (35)140
(36)151 (37)134 (38)143 (39)156 (40)160
(41)142 (42)139 (43)138 (44)147 (45)150
(46)134 (47)151 (48)160 (49)150 (50)149
(51)142 (52)130 (53)159 (54)151 (55)140
(56)151 (57)137 (58)154 (59)153 (60)145

Page 51, Item 1:

(1)1 (2)0 (3)25 (4)4 (5)8 (6)0 (7)5 (8)8
(9)2 (10)19 (11)5 (12)0 (13)8 (14)9 (15)14
(16)19 (17)1 (18)20 (19)20 (20)0 (21)15
(22)23 (23)1 (24)11 (25)7 (26)4 (27)6
(28)7 (29)26 (30)6 (31)13 (32)20 (33)16
(34)13 (35)26 (36)9 (37)20 (38)17 (39)10
(40)8 (41)15 (42)3 (43)10 (44)10 (45)3
(46)21 (47)2 (48)5 (49)20 (50)4 (51)10
(52)19 (53)19 (54)19 (55)16 (56)11 (57)2
(58)9 (59)4 (60)3

Page 52, Item 1:

(1)2 (2)3 (3)8 (4)20 (5)10 (6)2 (7)5 (8)0
(9)12 (10)10 (11)2 (12)15 (13)9 (14)4

(15)2 (16)11 (17)2 (18)14 (19)8 (20)5
(21)15 (22)6 (23)8 (24)5 (25)7 (26)1 (27)4
(28)3 (29)2 (30)16 (31)22 (32)17 (33)12
(34)12 (35)21 (36)3 (37)3 (38)15 (39)8
(40)5 (41)3 (42)11 (43)7 (44)17 (45)10
(46)8 (47)1 (48)11 (49)20 (50)3 (51)4
(52)4 (53)15 (54)2 (55)14 (56)3 (57)14
(58)23 (59)18 (60)21

Page 53, Item 1:
(1)7 (2)10 (3)26 (4)3 (5)0 (6)1 (7)9 (8)5
(9)1 (10)8 (11)15 (12)25 (13)0 (14)21
(15)13 (16)14 (17)11 (18)13 (19)4 (20)10
(21)10 (22)4 (23)5 (24)7 (25)5 (26)3 (27)7
(28)28 (29)18 (30)14 (31)12 (32)9 (33)6
(34)8 (35)5 (36)4 (37)30 (38)5 (39)5
(40)10 (41)6 (42)18 (43)25 (44)14 (45)15
(46)29 (47)13 (48)17 (49)21 (50)27 (51)1
(52)10 (53)13 (54)13 (55)1 (56)4 (57)15
(58)5 (59)20 (60)4

Page 54, Item 1:
(1)14 (2)6 (3)19 (4)20 (5)8 (6)5 (7)0 (8)12
(9)25 (10)1 (11)3 (12)18 (13)1 (14)24
(15)3 (16)21 (17)6 (18)1 (19)5 (20)3 (21)7
(22)13 (23)13 (24)5 (25)6 (26)0 (27)17
(28)13 (29)3 (30)3 (31)3 (32)4 (33)25
(34)15 (35)20 (36)21 (37)3 (38)4 (39)2
(40)17 (41)0 (42)4 (43)23 (44)9 (45)13
(46)6 (47)4 (48)4 (49)8 (50)3 (51)15 (52)5
(53)14 (54)12 (55)6 (56)10 (57)1 (58)13
(59)4 (60)1

Page 55, Item 1:
(1)4 (2)1 (3)2 (4)10 (5)2 (6)17 (7)6 (8)14
(9)7 (10)22 (11)0 (12)10 (13)17 (14)24
(15)13 (16)3 (17)12 (18)0 (19)5 (20)1
(21)8 (22)14 (23)6 (24)4 (25)9 (26)8 (27)9
(28)13 (29)17 (30)21 (31)9 (32)8 (33)8

(34)3 (35)23 (36)3 (37)26 (38)4 (39)12
(40)6 (41)21 (42)7 (43)19 (44)23 (45)12
(46)20 (47)14 (48)4 (49)11 (50)13 (51)4
(52)11 (53)3 (54)7 (55)15 (56)1 (57)4
(58)1 (59)8 (60)2

Page 56, Item 1:
(1)19 (2)18 (3)12 (4)25 (5)10 (6)35 (7)16
(8)29 (9)20 (10)36 (11)31 (12)35 (13)34
(14)37 (15)25 (16)19 (17)14 (18)17
(19)33 (20)24 (21)28 (22)15 (23)18
(24)28 (25)18 (26)35 (27)11 (28)31
(29)10 (30)31 (31)10 (32)36 (33)19
(34)35 (35)11 (36)33 (37)10 (38)32
(39)13 (40)31 (41)13 (42)31 (43)25
(44)32 (45)21 (46)35 (47)25 (48)40
(49)25 (50)19 (51)21 (52)27 (53)18
(54)35 (55)13 (56)34 (57)16 (58)37
(59)11 (60)38

Page 57, Item 1:
(1)11 (2)39 (3)29 (4)32 (5)21 (6)32 (7)19
(8)39 (9)15 (10)32 (11)22 (12)37 (13)19
(14)37 (15)29 (16)27 (17)11 (18)29
(19)36 (20)36 (21)23 (22)13 (23)13
(24)39 (25)21 (26)32 (27)16 (28)33
(29)12 (30)29 (31)28 (32)35 (33)26
(34)10 (35)30 (36)30 (37)14 (38)40
(39)19 (40)17 (41)22 (42)36 (43)30
(44)36 (45)13 (46)27 (47)18 (48)17
(49)16 (50)38 (51)22 (52)33 (53)37
(54)35 (55)37 (56)40 (57)21 (58)29
(59)12 (60)21

Page 58, Item 1:

(1)16 (2)36 (3)10 (4)36 (5)24 (6)39 (7)28
(8)16 (9)13 (10)27 (11)28 (12)34 (13)29
(14)30 (15)12 (16)29 (17)12 (18)34
(19)11 (20)29 (21)26 (22)28 (23)29
(24)14 (25)21 (26)23 (27)14 (28)22
(29)38 (30)34 (31)11 (32)32 (33)22
(34)26 (35)12 (36)24 (37)31 (38)38
(39)31 (40)40 (41)24 (42)36 (43)17
(44)23 (45)29 (46)21 (47)20 (48)35
(49)14 (50)31 (51)26 (52)15 (53)15
(54)11 (55)10 (56)38 (57)35 (58)28
(59)20 (60)39

Page 59, Item 1:

(1)23 (2)36 (3)28 (4)33 (5)14 (6)32 (7)14
(8)34 (9)31 (10)34 (11)22 (12)40 (13)18
(14)36 (15)26 (16)28 (17)12 (18)38
(19)12 (20)34 (21)10 (22)34 (23)11
(24)38 (25)15 (26)39 (27)24 (28)15
(29)28 (30)40 (31)18 (32)31 (33)19
(34)31 (35)12 (36)37 (37)23 (38)36
(39)32 (40)22 (41)27 (42)29 (43)14
(44)40 (45)10 (46)37 (47)15 (48)23
(49)12 (50)27 (51)16 (52)28 (53)30
(54)36 (55)13 (56)33 (57)18 (58)39
(59)23 (60)37

Page 60, Item 1:

(1)12 (2)40 (3)12 (4)27 (5)16 (6)40 (7)39
(8)37 (9)20 (10)30 (11)26 (12)26 (13)12
(14)19 (15)10 (16)11 (17)21 (18)36
(19)11 (20)38 (21)32 (22)18 (23)10
(24)36 (25)29 (26)35 (27)23 (28)17
(29)23 (30)29 (31)21 (32)40 (33)12
(34)37 (35)11 (36)31 (37)23 (38)30
(39)32 (40)40 (41)17 (42)24 (43)38
(44)40 (45)12 (46)26 (47)21 (48)24

(49)29 (50)38 (51)18 (52)21 (53)12
(54)21 (55)28 (56)30 (57)14 (58)26
(59)26 (60)31

Page 61, Item 1:

(1)24 (2)5 (3)3 (4)3 (5)14 (6)0 (7)17 (8)2
(9)3 (10)0 (11)0 (12)22 (13)5 (14)18
(15)16 (16)7 (17)0 (18)13 (19)12 (20)3
(21)1 (22)9 (23)8 (24)11 (25)14 (26)5
(27)5 (28)10 (29)3 (30)13 (31)15 (32)27
(33)10 (34)19 (35)0 (36)15 (37)15 (38)22
(39)17 (40)11 (41)25 (42)3 (43)6 (44)18
(45)14 (46)3 (47)2 (48)22 (49)19 (50)0
(51)18 (52)7 (53)1 (54)5 (55)1 (56)4 (57)5
(58)2 (59)18 (60)8

Page 62, Item 1:

(1)4 (2)9 (3)28 (4)21 (5)7 (6)12 (7)22
(8)12 (9)6 (10)6 (11)1 (12)5 (13)5 (14)2
(15)6 (16)0 (17)13 (18)12 (19)2 (20)18
(21)22 (22)0 (23)3 (24)1 (25)5 (26)8
(27)29 (28)5 (29)0 (30)6 (31)12 (32)6
(33)10 (34)5 (35)4 (36)0 (37)10 (38)16
(39)6 (40)1 (41)1 (42)4 (43)10 (44)25
(45)7 (46)4 (47)8 (48)7 (49)4 (50)5 (51)18
(52)3 (53)1 (54)6 (55)7 (56)5 (57)5 (58)19
(59)2 (60)2

Page 63, Item 1:

(1)11 (2)7 (3)3 (4)0 (5)10 (6)3 (7)4 (8)17
(9)3 (10)9 (11)11 (12)9 (13)8 (14)4 (15)30
(16)4 (17)17 (18)1 (19)6 (20)1 (21)25
(22)12 (23)8 (24)2 (25)10 (26)11 (27)7
(28)3 (29)5 (30)25 (31)7 (32)2 (33)6
(34)12 (35)3 (36)3 (37)18 (38)3 (39)4

(40)4 (41)11 (42)1 (43)12 (44)4 (45)7
(46)5 (47)2 (48)6 (49)2 (50)14 (51)8 (52)1
(53)1 (54)4 (55)10 (56)22 (57)16 (58)6
(59)5 (60)2

Page 64, Item 1:
(1)22 (2)15 (3)26 (4)14 (5)6 (6)12 (7)4
(8)16 (9)4 (10)5 (11)11 (12)11 (13)2
(14)17 (15)11 (16)7 (17)11 (18)7 (19)6
(20)5 (21)13 (22)5 (23)8 (24)4 (25)7
(26)18 (27)2 (28)11 (29)4 (30)1 (31)9
(32)0 (33)7 (34)1 (35)4 (36)2 (37)1 (38)4
(39)5 (40)13 (41)4 (42)3 (43)21 (44)10
(45)14 (46)24 (47)19 (48)8 (49)8 (50)5
(51)10 (52)14 (53)18 (54)8 (55)11 (56)16
(57)12 (58)1 (59)2 (60)5

Page 65, Item 1:
(1)10 (2)3 (3)18 (4)16 (5)15 (6)5 (7)21
(8)5 (9)2 (10)11 (11)1 (12)7 (13)15 (14)6
(15)1 (16)13 (17)2 (18)7 (19)5 (20)15
(21)24 (22)15 (23)29 (24)10 (25)22
(26)10 (27)18 (28)9 (29)2 (30)12 (31)21
(32)15 (33)12 (34)6 (35)27 (36)20 (37)10
(38)26 (39)25 (40)15 (41)7 (42)22 (43)21
(44)11 (45)21 (46)19 (47)16 (48)4 (49)9
(50)9 (51)1 (52)4 (53)21 (54)0 (55)26
(56)0 (57)27 (58)15 (59)0 (60)8

Page 66, Item 1:
(1)51 (2)70 (3)61 (4)61 (5)44 (6)47 (7)53
(8)64 (9)51 (10)66 (11)40 (12)53 (13)57
(14)70 (15)58 (16)58 (17)50 (18)59
(19)41 (20)44 (21)48 (22)48 (23)41
(24)68 (25)69 (26)46 (27)55 (28)58
(29)41 (30)68 (31)49 (32)60 (33)41
(34)70 (35)61 (36)66 (37)51 (38)70
(39)64 (40)63 (41)68 (42)43 (43)45
(44)61 (45)55 (46)59 (47)59 (48)56

(49)57 (50)70 (51)48 (52)65 (53)54
(54)65 (55)43 (56)61 (57)51 (58)63
(59)46 (60)62
Page 67, Item 1:
(1)48 (2)63 (3)47 (4)58 (5)58 (6)58 (7)43
(8)58 (9)40 (10)45 (11)61 (12)59 (13)48
(14)70 (15)46 (16)51 (17)46 (18)52
(19)50 (20)65 (21)47 (22)52 (23)41
(24)56 (25)67 (26)56 (27)46 (28)67
(29)57 (30)56 (31)58 (32)57 (33)68
(34)48 (35)55 (36)58 (37)40 (38)60
(39)41 (40)62 (41)41 (42)67 (43)43
(44)66 (45)49 (46)54 (47)49 (48)63
(49)40 (50)55 (51)41 (52)53 (53)50
(54)50 (55)47 (56)68 (57)48 (58)48
(59)49 (60)54

Page 68, Item 1:
(1)49 (2)52 (3)49 (4)69 (5)45 (6)65 (7)52
(8)63 (9)57 (10)50 (11)60 (12)68 (13)44
(14)59 (15)58 (16)51 (17)48 (18)69
(19)40 (20)70 (21)65 (22)69 (23)47
(24)70 (25)50 (26)62 (27)40 (28)59
(29)40 (30)68 (31)45 (32)59 (33)44
(34)52 (35)50 (36)67 (37)44 (38)57
(39)54 (40)51 (41)49 (42)45 (43)40
(44)66 (45)46 (46)46 (47)64 (48)61
(49)68 (50)57 (51)62 (52)65 (53)40
(54)57 (55)47 (56)68 (57)49 (58)66
(59)52 (60)50
Page 69, Item 1:
(1)56 (2)61 (3)65 (4)65 (5)40 (6)55 (7)60
(8)57 (9)42 (10)63 (11)51 (12)63 (13)44
(14)66 (15)58 (16)66 (17)51 (18)57
(19)45

(20)45 (21)44 (22)67 (23)47 (24)64
(25)50 (26)60 (27)40 (28)49 (29)42
(30)53 (31)48 (32)62 (33)51 (34)66
(35)42 (36)70 (37)61 (38)68 (39)48
(40)70 (41)65 (42)55 (43)60 (44)63
(45)44 (46)59 (47)44 (48)55 (49)50
(50)66 (51)53 (52)63 (53)54 (54)56
(55)42 (56)70 (57)42 (58)69 (59)44
(60)62

Page 70, Item 1:
(1)46 (2)54 (3)53 (4)50 (5)49 (6)63 (7)44
(8)56 (9)45 (10)67 (11)49 (12)66 (13)47
(14)48 (15)45 (16)50 (17)67 (18)42
(19)57 (20)70 (21)44 (22)62 (23)44
(24)61 (25)60 (26)49 (27)65 (28)68
(29)57 (30)61 (31)53 (32)66 (33)45
(34)65 (35)48 (36)61 (37)45 (38)49
(39)41 (40)68 (41)60 (42)69 (43)53
(44)57 (45)41 (46)64 (47)58 (48)70
(49)42 (50)60 (51)44 (52)53 (53)63
(54)62 (55)60 (56)67 (57)42 (58)58
(59)51 (60)68

Page 71, Item 1:
(1)1 (2)0 (3)2 (4)9 (5)16 (6)20 (7)5 (8)8
(9)6 (10)0 (11)6 (12)22 (13)9 (14)29 (15)1
(16)17 (17)10 (18)3 (19)10 (20)15 (21)0
(22)13 (23)9 (24)18 (25)3 (26)21 (27)14
(28)19 (29)19 (30)7 (31)1 (32)2 (33)22
(34)20 (35)7 (36)16 (37)18 (38)18 (39)0
(40)4 (41)4 (42)18 (43)4 (44)19 (45)6
(46)8 (47)14 (48)5 (49)1 (50)15 (51)20
(52)18 (53)3 (54)3 (55)0 (56)14 (57)1
(58)10 (59)0 (60)5

Page 72, Item 1:
(1)3 (2)16 (3)20 (4)0 (5)1 (6)0 (7)1 (8)6
(9)4 (10)6 (11)16 (12)12 (13)7 (14)22

(15)12 (16)9 (17)26 (18)10 (19)7 (20)4
(21)13 (22)3 (23)27 (24)5 (25)3 (26)12
(27)8 (28)12 (29)8 (30)1 (31)7 (32)27
(33)17 (34)22 (35)2 (36)22 (37)7 (38)13
(39)22 (40)4 (41)9 (42)20 (43)14 (44)7
(45)20 (46)5 (47)17 (48)12 (49)5 (50)29
(51)19 (52)14 (53)14 (54)9 (55)14 (56)3
(57)4 (58)1 (59)1 (60)5

Page 73, Item 1:
(1)1 (2)27 (3)22 (4)1 (5)22 (6)8 (7)8 (8)4
(9)30 (10)2 (11)5 (12)6 (13)4 (14)10 (15)0
(16)14 (17)4 (18)19 (19)14 (20)4 (21)1
(22)14 (23)13 (24)0 (25)4 (26)3 (27)0
(28)8 (29)9 (30)24 (31)16 (32)26 (33)5
(34)23 (35)14 (36)4 (37)12 (38)8 (39)0
(40)14 (41)10 (42)8 (43)8 (44)5 (45)1
(46)13 (47)23 (48)5 (49)4 (50)18 (51)24
(52)7 (53)3 (54)3 (55)3 (56)5 (57)6 (58)3
(59)14 (60)0

Page 74, Item 1:
(1)13 (2)7 (3)13 (4)16 (5)2 (6)6 (7)6 (8)9
(9)3 (10)5 (11)4 (12)0 (13)13 (14)23
(15)22 (16)3 (17)4 (18)1 (19)12 (20)7
(21)0 (22)3 (23)5 (24)0 (25)11 (26)3 (27)5
(28)8 (29)4 (30)8 (31)9 (32)6 (33)17 (34)9
(35)13 (36)7 (37)13 (38)29 (39)22 (40)4
(41)13 (42)4 (43)10 (44)9 (45)4 (46)2
(47)0 (48)8 (49)3 (50)8 (51)0 (52)13
(53)19 (54)2 (55)8 (56)13 (57)17 (58)14
(59)21 (60)4

Page 75, Item 1:

(1)5 (2)16 (3)0 (4)1 (5)23 (6)20 (7)9 (8)25
(9)13 (10)0 (11)3 (12)27 (13)2 (14)5 (15)9
(16)0 (17)0 (18)10 (19)2 (20)12 (21)28
(22)17 (23)26 (24)18 (25)6 (26)12 (27)3
(28)7 (29)16 (30)0 (31)4 (32)0 (33)4
(34)18 (35)19 (36)16 (37)19 (38)3 (39)13
(40)23 (41)3 (42)8 (43)2 (44)8 (45)3 (46)4
(47)19 (48)6 (49)16 (50)9 (51)26 (52)7
(53)18 (54)0 (55)27 (56)1 (57)9 (58)14
(59)15 (60)2

Page 76, Item 1:

(1)75 (2)85 (3)81 (4)73 (5)88 (6)90 (7)71
(8)95 (9)75 (10)91 (11)94 (12)82 (13)71
(14)89 (15)92 (16)100 (17)73 (18)99
(19)95 (20)84 (21)71 (22)92 (23)78
(24)94 (25)91 (26)96 (27)77 (28)90
(29)90 (30)87 (31)72 (32)96 (33)74
(34)99 (35)70 (36)91 (37)74 (38)76
(39)72 (40)76 (41)84 (42)87 (43)80
(44)92 (45)98 (46)88 (47)92 (48)79
(49)73 (50)90 (51)95 (52)84 (53)78
(54)81 (55)90 (56)93 (57)87 (58)88
(59)79 (60)95

Page 77, Item 1:

(1)81 (2)72 (3)73 (4)74 (5)73 (6)81 (7)74
(8)90 (9)90 (10)83 (11)98 (12)89 (13)94
(14)91 (15)92 (16)91 (17)78 (18)98
(19)81 (20)99 (21)93 (22)99 (23)85
(24)100 (25)76 (26)80 (27)91 (28)81
(29)89 (30)92 (31)86 (32)99 (33)74
(34)82 (35)83 (36)74 (37)83 (38)82
(39)83 (40)90 (41)74 (42)86 (43)83
(44)92 (45)72 (46)77 (47)73 (48)88
(49)79 (50)96 (51)72 (52)100 (53)70
(54)77 (55)94 (56)90 (57)70 (58)94
(59)79 (60)97

Page 78, Item 1:

(1)76 (2)97 (3)87 (4)89 (5)77 (6)98 (7)71
(8)93 (9)72 (10)91 (11)77 (12)87 (13)96
(14)88 (15)75 (16)80 (17)71 (18)78
(19)80 (20)100 (21)81 (22)97 (23)79
(24)96 (25)70 (26)83 (27)97 (28)81
(29)83 (30)92 (31)98 (32)83 (33)81
(34)98 (35)92 (36)94 (37)85 (38)83
(39)82 (40)86 (41)76 (42)87 (43)74
(44)98 (45)76 (46)80 (47)87 (48)97
(49)79 (50)94 (51)75 (52)98 (53)72
(54)96 (55)75 (56)98 (57)100 (58)79
(59)94 (60)97

Page 79, Item 1:

(1)78 (2)78 (3)81 (4)98 (5)82 (6)88 (7)86
(8)97 (9)73 (10)82 (11)80 (12)100 (13)73
(14)92 (15)83 (16)92 (17)70 (18)92
(19)78 (20)93 (21)79 (22)92 (23)79
(24)89 (25)70 (26)96 (27)84 (28)97
(29)86 (30)96 (31)80 (32)91 (33)77
(34)87 (35)71 (36)94 (37)90 (38)95
(39)80 (40)83 (41)83 (42)94 (43)76
(44)99 (45)73 (46)98 (47)76 (48)90
(49)70 (50)92 (51)76 (52)87 (53)75
(54)85 (55)71 (56)95 (57)80 (58)78
(59)71 (60)90

Page 80, Item 1:

(1)74 (2)80 (3)86 (4)80 (5)95 (6)99 (7)93
(8)88 (9)81 (10)93 (11)94 (12)92 (13)81
(14)86 (15)81 (16)91 (17)81 (18)100
(19)71 (20)79 (21)85 (22)84 (23)78
(24)99 (25)75 (26)98 (27)73 (28)99
(29)77 (30)94 (31)76 (32)96 (33)80
(34)92 (35)73 (36)97

(37)74 (38)95 (39)70 (40)77 (41)79
(42)82 (43)85 (44)83 (45)72 (46)93
(47)76 (48)91 (49)78 (50)96 (51)76
(52)94 (53)70 (54)99 (55)77 (56)92
(57)88 (58)92 (59)72 (60)95

Page 81, Item 1:

(1)19 (2)13 (3)4 (4)4 (5)14 (6)14 (7)13
(8)4 (9)22 (10)16 (11)17 (12)5 (13)21
(14)5 (15)19 (16)0 (17)25 (18)19 (19)15
(20)10 (21)22 (22)3 (23)3 (24)21 (25)11
(26)20 (27)23 (28)1 (29)13 (30)12 (31)6
(32)17 (33)8 (34)1 (35)0 (36)15 (37)21
(38)11 (39)6 (40)14 (41)11 (42)11 (43)9
(44)24 (45)7 (46)14 (47)4 (48)5 (49)12
(50)26 (51)26 (52)0 (53)6 (54)17 (55)24
(56)8 (57)8 (58)7 (59)4 (60)8

Page 82, Item 1:

(1)5 (2)8 (3)6 (4)2 (5)1 (6)9 (7)10 (8)23
(9)7 (10)7 (11)1 (12)0 (13)2 (14)0 (15)15
(16)21 (17)0 (18)13 (19)20 (20)10 (21)12
(22)11 (23)7 (24)8 (25)4 (26)21 (27)17
(28)3 (29)27 (30)10 (31)11 (32)0 (33)15
(34)21 (35)2 (36)1 (37)15 (38)2 (39)5
(40)19 (41)21 (42)1 (43)14 (44)24 (45)0
(46)0 (47)10 (48)22 (49)3 (50)5 (51)8
(52)9 (53)7 (54)6 (55)5 (56)14 (57)7 (58)1
(59)15 (60)20

Page 83, Item 1:

(1)15 (2)16 (3)5 (4)7 (5)10 (6)9 (7)2 (8)2
(9)3 (10)11 (11)19 (12)23 (13)6 (14)19
(15)6 (16)4 (17)15 (18)13 (19)7 (20)2
(21)11 (22)7 (23)0 (24)9 (25)28 (26)23
(27)26 (28)11 (29)5 (30)13 (31)7 (32)4
(33)2 (34)3 (35)0 (36)6 (37)1 (38)19 (39)7
(40)5 (41)0 (42)7 (43)12 (44)8 (45)2 (46)6
(47)2 (48)9 (49)8 (50)14 (51)9 (52)6 (53)7

(54)2 (55)19 (56)17 (57)15 (58)12 (59)0
(60)18

Page 84, Item 1:

(1)22 (2)1 (3)10 (4)8 (5)6 (6)19 (7)1 (8)9
(9)4 (10)9 (11)18 (12)5 (13)13 (14)0
(15)14 (16)5 (17)20 (18)2 (19)9 (20)6
(21)23 (22)10 (23)2 (24)3 (25)10 (26)12
(27)0 (28)0 (29)14 (30)3 (31)13 (32)6
(33)5 (34)21 (35)2 (36)15 (37)22 (38)21
(39)6 (40)5 (41)14 (42)15 (43)6 (44)1
(45)11 (46)11 (47)2 (48)14 (49)0 (50)14
(51)20 (52)0 (53)3 (54)14 (55)3 (56)8
(57)10 (58)19 (59)16 (60)0

Page 85, Item 1:

(1)30 (2)8 (3)24 (4)1 (5)6 (6)3 (7)0 (8)0
(9)3 (10)0 (11)17 (12)12 (13)0 (14)9
(15)12 (16)2 (17)1 (18)2 (19)6 (20)0 (21)1
(22)9 (23)3 (24)15 (25)13 (26)9 (27)17
(28)18 (29)17 (30)15 (31)17 (32)6 (33)10
(34)6 (35)15 (36)16 (37)10 (38)10 (39)0
(40)2 (41)5 (42)4 (43)18 (44)11 (45)27
(46)29 (47)1 (48)3 (49)14 (50)19 (51)0
(52)1 (53)4 (54)19 (55)20 (56)6 (57)14
(58)18 (59)0 (60)12

Page 86, Item 1:

(1)108 (2)111 (3)100 (4)121 (5)103
(6)111 (7)113 (8)114 (9)113 (10)130
(11)110 (12)130 (13)102 (14)105 (15)114
(16)122 (17)100 (18)119 (19)120 (20)114
(21)112

(22)116 (23)106 (24)127 (25)108 (26)126
(27)115 (28)121 (29)108 (30)108 (31)105
(32)121 (33)107 (34)106 (35)101 (36)128
(37)121 (38)113 (39)100 (40)112 (41)104
(42)106 (43)121 (44)118 (45)101 (46)123
(47)122 (48)124 (49)105 (50)129 (51)116
(52)126 (53)127 (54)110 (55)102 (56)111
(57)111 (58)123 (59)100 (60)117
Page 87, Item 1:
(1)114 (2)122 (3)106 (4)120 (5)114
(6)115 (7)108 (8)125 (9)104 (10)123
(11)126 (12)115 (13)100 (14)124 (15)111
(16)122 (17)126 (18)126 (19)110 (20)129
(21)101 (22)111 (23)113 (24)121 (25)101
(26)116 (27)111 (28)119 (29)102 (30)120
(31)115 (32)117 (33)105 (34)107 (35)108
(36)124 (37)107 (38)127 (39)121 (40)127
(41)118 (42)128 (43)100 (44)129 (45)109
(46)123 (47)103 (48)119 (49)106 (50)118
(51)105 (52)122 (53)112 (54)126 (55)108
(56)117 (57)111 (58)125 (59)123 (60)111
Page 88, Item 1:
(1)109 (2)123 (3)101 (4)118 (5)119
(6)112 (7)106 (8)117 (9)102 (10)126
(11)116 (12)127 (13)118 (14)125 (15)108
(16)126 (17)111 (18)124 (19)116 (20)127
(21)105 (22)105 (23)119 (24)126 (25)105
(26)129 (27)120 (28)123 (29)104 (30)121
(31)100 (32)108 (33)105 (34)122 (35)115
(36)125 (37)103 (38)125 (39)106 (40)130
(41)114 (42)113 (43)102 (44)116 (45)118
(46)130 (47)119 (48)117 (49)126 (50)127
(51)103 (52)128 (53)100 (54)115 (55)106
(56)113 (57)111 (58)121 (59)103 (60)117
Page 89, Item 1:
(1)127 (2)114 (3)118 (4)128 (5)110

(6)118 (7)105 (8)104 (9)111 (10)110
(11)102 (12)121 (13)111 (14)123 (15)105
(16)124 (17)120 (18)130 (19)104 (20)121
(21)122 (22)122 (23)110 (24)129 (25)102
(26)119 (27)119 (28)128 (29)114 (30)129
(31)101 (32)130 (33)116 (34)124 (35)104
(36)124 (37)113 (38)128 (39)108 (40)105
(41)101 (42)114 (43)102 (44)119 (45)114
(46)120 (47)110 (48)113 (49)103 (50)115
(51)118 (52)120 (53)107 (54)130 (55)110
(56)127 (57)114 (58)112 (59)119 (60)123
Page 90, Item 1:
(1)114 (2)129 (3)105 (4)121 (5)104
(6)108 (7)102 (8)125 (9)128 (10)107
(11)104 (12)122 (13)108 (14)130 (15)101
(16)129 (17)104 (18)122 (19)125 (20)129
(21)100 (22)103 (23)122 (24)129 (25)127
(26)107 (27)118 (28)111 (29)109 (30)129
(31)103 (32)125 (33)117 (34)122 (35)100
(36)124 (37)125 (38)110 (39)109 (40)123
(41)104 (42)122 (43)112 (44)126 (45)104
(46)115 (47)103 (48)126 (49)105 (50)128
(51)105 (52)118 (53)110 (54)128 (55)100
(56)114 (57)115 (58)119 (59)115 (60)130
Page 91, Item 1:
(1)3 (2)1 (3)2 (4)1 (5)24 (6)3 (7)18 (8)21
(9)24 (10)12 (11)10 (12)19 (13)4 (14)1

(15)3 (16)10 (17)14 (18)4 (19)3 (20)10
(21)15 (22)14 (23)25 (24)8 (25)15 (26)3
(27)5 (28)14 (29)22 (30)10 (31)2 (32)7
(33)14 (34)0 (35)16 (36)18 (37)1 (38)5
(39)5 (40)21 (41)7 (42)0 (43)3 (44)4
(45)10 (46)6 (47)0 (48)2 (49)12 (50)12
(51)9 (52)7 (53)13 (54)0 (55)6 (56)19
(57)8 (58)4 (59)9 (60)26

Page 92, Item 1:

(1)19 (2)26 (3)9 (4)18 (5)7 (6)3 (7)20 (8)9
(9)13 (10)2 (11)6 (12)9 (13)11 (14)28
(15)6 (16)5 (17)15 (18)1 (19)1 (20)7 (21)5
(22)0 (23)6 (24)3 (25)1 (26)3 (27)11
(28)21 (29)8 (30)13 (31)11 (32)21 (33)4
(34)6 (35)13 (36)5 (37)13 (38)1 (39)4
(40)17 (41)10 (42)0 (43)16 (44)3 (45)10
(46)6 (47)0 (48)9 (49)12 (50)23 (51)20
(52)6 (53)11 (54)8 (55)15 (56)2 (57)14
(58)15 (59)15 (60)8

Page 93, Item 1:

(1)7 (2)16 (3)19 (4)24 (5)13 (6)15 (7)3
(8)4 (9)16 (10)9 (11)2 (12)20 (13)8 (14)5
(15)4 (16)3 (17)1 (18)9 (19)17 (20)22
(21)3 (22)17 (23)29 (24)12 (25)5 (26)6
(27)0 (28)2 (29)8 (30)10 (31)9 (32)1 (33)8
(34)2 (35)21 (36)12 (37)4 (38)6 (39)19
(40)23 (41)0 (42)12 (43)7 (44)6 (45)9
(46)2 (47)10 (48)28 (49)3 (50)0 (51)10
(52)15 (53)0 (54)12 (55)15 (56)6 (57)3
(58)0 (59)0 (60)1

Page 94, Item 1:

(1)16 (2)15 (3)4 (4)4 (5)10 (6)5 (7)22 (8)0
(9)13 (10)0 (11)0 (12)13 (13)2 (14)19
(15)0 (16)19 (17)23 (18)23 (19)21 (20)7
(21)8 (22)23 (23)12 (24)1 (25)12 (26)5
(27)0 (28)22 (29)2 (30)4 (31)11 (32)11

(33)6 (34)14 (35)13 (36)15 (37)3 (38)1
(39)0 (40)15 (41)17 (42)2 (43)11 (44)27
(45)0 (46)0 (47)6 (48)19 (49)27 (50)8
(51)17 (52)23 (53)11 (54)4 (55)12 (56)6
(57)7 (58)19 (59)15 (60)16

Page 95, Item 1:

(1)23 (2)5 (3)9 (4)17 (5)0 (6)7 (7)4 (8)19
(9)1 (10)6 (11)1 (12)8 (13)0 (14)18 (15)14
(16)4 (17)18 (18)14 (19)2 (20)5 (21)5
(22)8 (23)0 (24)1 (25)2 (26)0 (27)16 (28)4
(29)14 (30)9 (31)21 (32)18 (33)26 (34)17
(35)1 (36)3 (37)7 (38)10 (39)9 (40)2 (41)8
(42)9 (43)8 (44)11 (45)9 (46)7 (47)26
(48)10 (49)15 (50)11 (51)4 (52)18 (53)16
(54)8 (55)11 (56)1 (57)8 (58)1 (59)10
(60)16

Page 96, Item 1:

(1)130 (2)146 (3)139 (4)147 (5)146
(6)155 (7)154 (8)132 (9)132 (10)160
(11)134 (12)159 (13)148 (14)133 (15)141
(16)148 (17)146 (18)151 (19)158 (20)158
(21)133 (22)151 (23)142 (24)149 (25)133
(26)137 (27)130 (28)146 (29)134 (30)157
(31)142 (32)147 (33)148 (34)146 (35)130
(36)137 (37)135 (38)155 (39)150 (40)149
(41)137 (42)149 (43)131 (44)158 (45)131
(46)138 (47)130 (48)153 (49)136 (50)148
(51)156

(52)153 (53)140 (54)159 (55)136 (56)157
(57)155 (58)158 (59)139 (60)145
Page 97, Item 1:
(1)139 (2)147 (3)141 (4)155 (5)138
(6)145 (7)142 (8)135 (9)132 (10)133
(11)144 (12)144 (13)145 (14)142 (15)147
(16)145 (17)140 (18)142 (19)130 (20)150
(21)146 (22)151 (23)146 (24)137 (25)145
(26)138 (27)133 (28)158 (29)158 (30)145
(31)139 (32)133 (33)154 (34)154 (35)140
(36)155 (37)141 (38)146 (39)135 (40)150
(41)151 (42)156 (43)135 (44)152 (45)136
(46)158 (47)140 (48)153 (49)140 (50)159
(51)132 (52)135 (53)142 (54)158 (55)152
(56)160 (57)141 (58)152 (59)143 (60)148
Page 98, Item 1:
(1)134 (2)147 (3)130 (4)158 (5)140
(6)152 (7)134 (8)149 (9)130 (10)158
(11)134 (12)136 (13)131 (14)154 (15)138
(16)143 (17)143 (18)157 (19)131 (20)139
(21)138 (22)144 (23)133 (24)147 (25)142
(26)146 (27)154 (28)139 (29)147 (30)160
(31)144 (32)154 (33)142 (34)146 (35)148
(36)159 (37)140 (38)151 (39)138 (40)150
(41)145 (42)154 (43)149 (44)156 (45)131
(46)154 (47)138 (48)150 (49)154 (50)160
(51)132 (52)147 (53)131 (54)152 (55)136
(56)153 (57)141 (58)154 (59)150 (60)138
Page 99, Item 1:
(1)130 (2)148 (3)141 (4)138 (5)144
(6)154 (7)137 (8)143 (9)140 (10)151
(11)134 (12)156 (13)148 (14)131 (15)144
(16)156 (17)134 (18)158 (19)151 (20)158
(21)146 (22)147 (23)141 (24)154 (25)140
(26)141 (27)146 (28)158 (29)141 (30)159
(31)133 (32)149 (33)142 (34)144 (35)131

(36)154 (37)152 (38)153 (39)132 (40)137
(41)133 (42)137 (43)138 (44)145 (45)145
(46)135 (47)146 (48)148 (49)159 (50)156
(51)140 (52)144 (53)141 (54)160 (55)134
(56)156 (57)141 (58)151 (59)131 (60)159
Page 100, Item 1:
(1)138 (2)160 (3)133 (4)146 (5)141
(6)157 (7)143 (8)156 (9)136 (10)148
(11)152 (12)158 (13)150 (14)155 (15)153
(16)153 (17)133 (18)156 (19)131 (20)149
(21)130 (22)158 (23)147 (24)155 (25)130
(26)152 (27)134 (28)137 (29)131 (30)140
(31)142 (32)151 (33)142 (34)138 (35)145
(36)152 (37)142 (38)154 (39)147 (40)141
(41)132 (42)153 (43)142 (44)159 (45)133
(46)154 (47)156 (48)150 (49)136 (50)146
(51)152 (52)147 (53)139 (54)135 (55)132
(56)156 (57)131 (58)155 (59)135 (60)156

PAPER CROW